T0084881

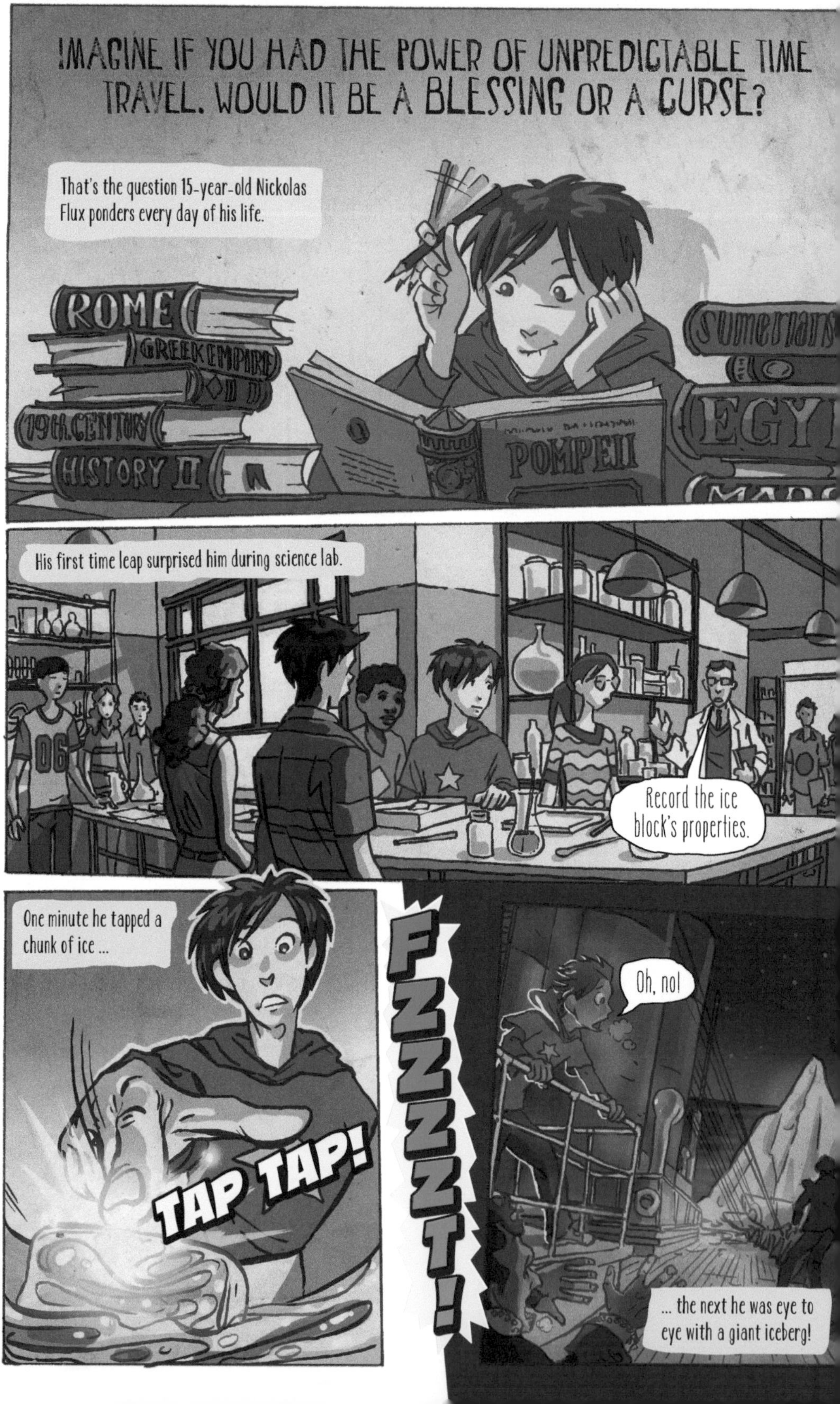
IMAGINE IF YOU HAD THE POWER OF UNPREDICTABLE TIME TRAVEL. WOULD IT BE A BLESSING OR A CURSE?
That's the question 15-year-old Nickolas Flux ponders every day of his life.
ROME
GREEK EMPIRE
19th CENTURY
HISTORY II
POMPEII
His first time leap surprised him during science lab.
Record the ice block's properties.
One minute he tapped a chunk of ice ...
TAP TAP!
FZZZZT!
Oh, no!
... the next he was eye to eye with a giant iceberg!

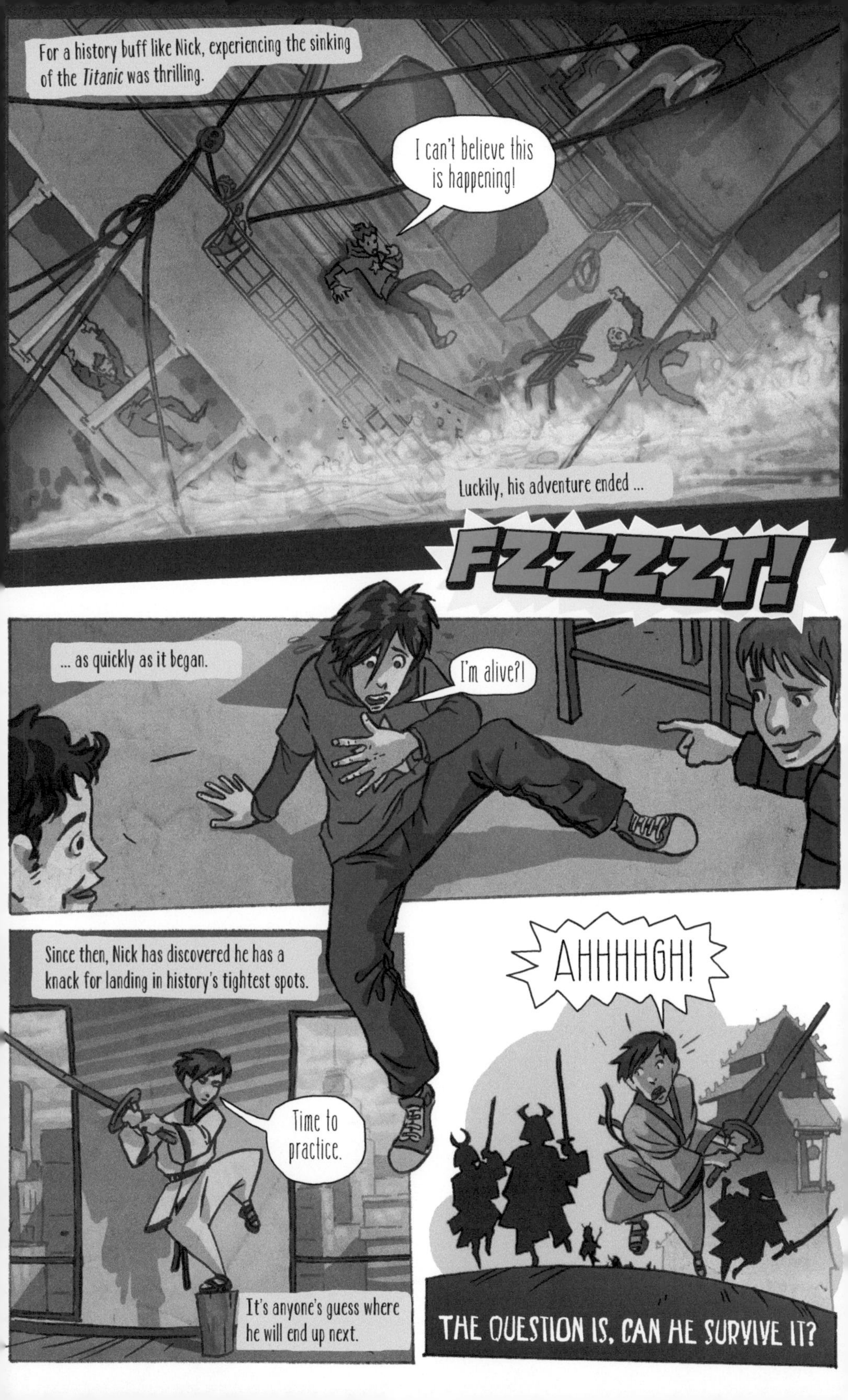
For a history buff like Nick, experiencing the sinking of the *Titanic* was thrilling.
I can't believe this is happening!
Luckily, his adventure ended ...
FZZZZT!
... as quickly as it began.
I'm alive?!
Since then, Nick has discovered he has a knack for landing in history's tightest spots.
Time to practice.
It's anyone's guess where he will end up next.
AHHHHGH!
THE QUESTION IS, CAN HE SURVIVE IT?

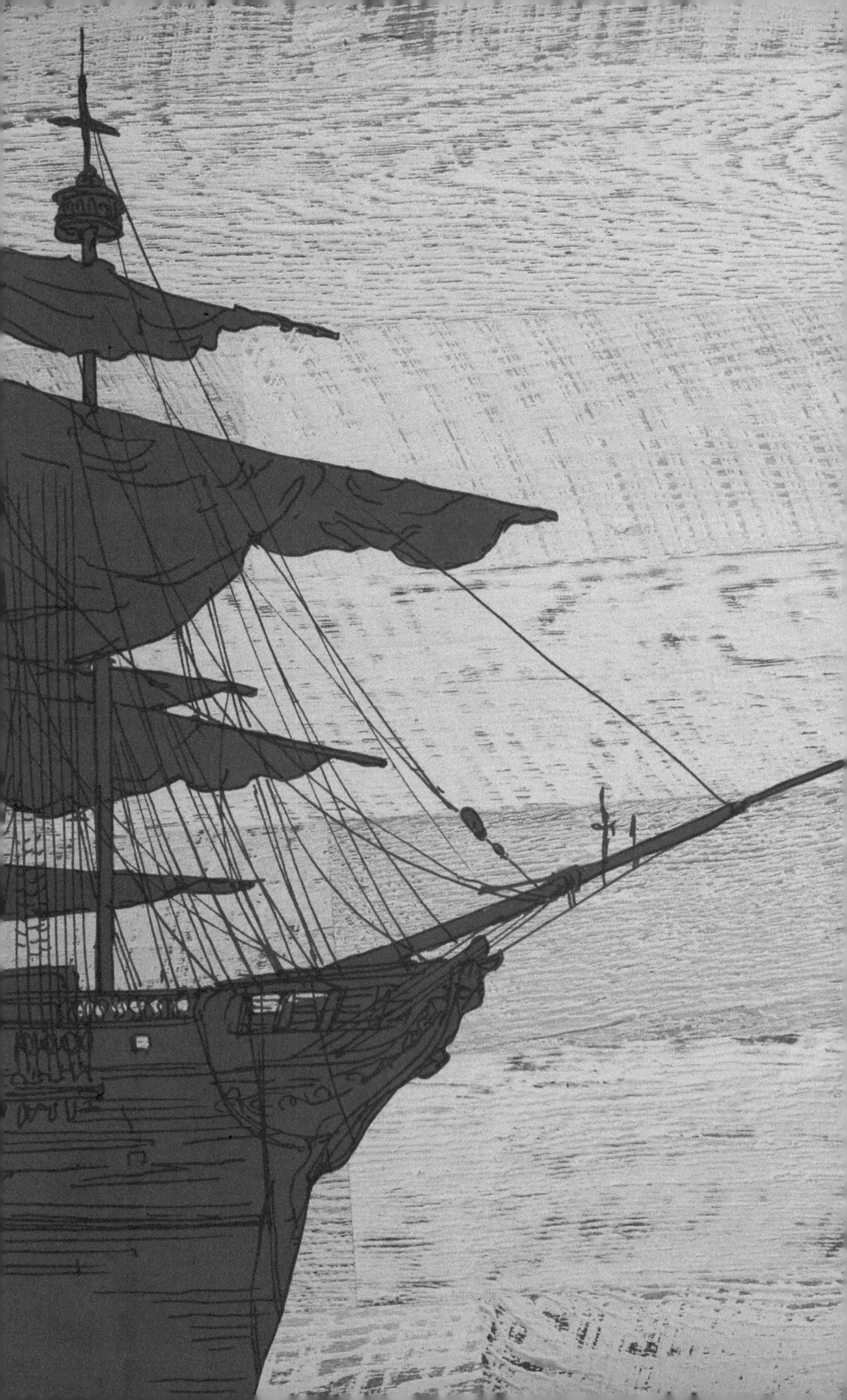

Nickolas Flux HISTORY CHRONICLES

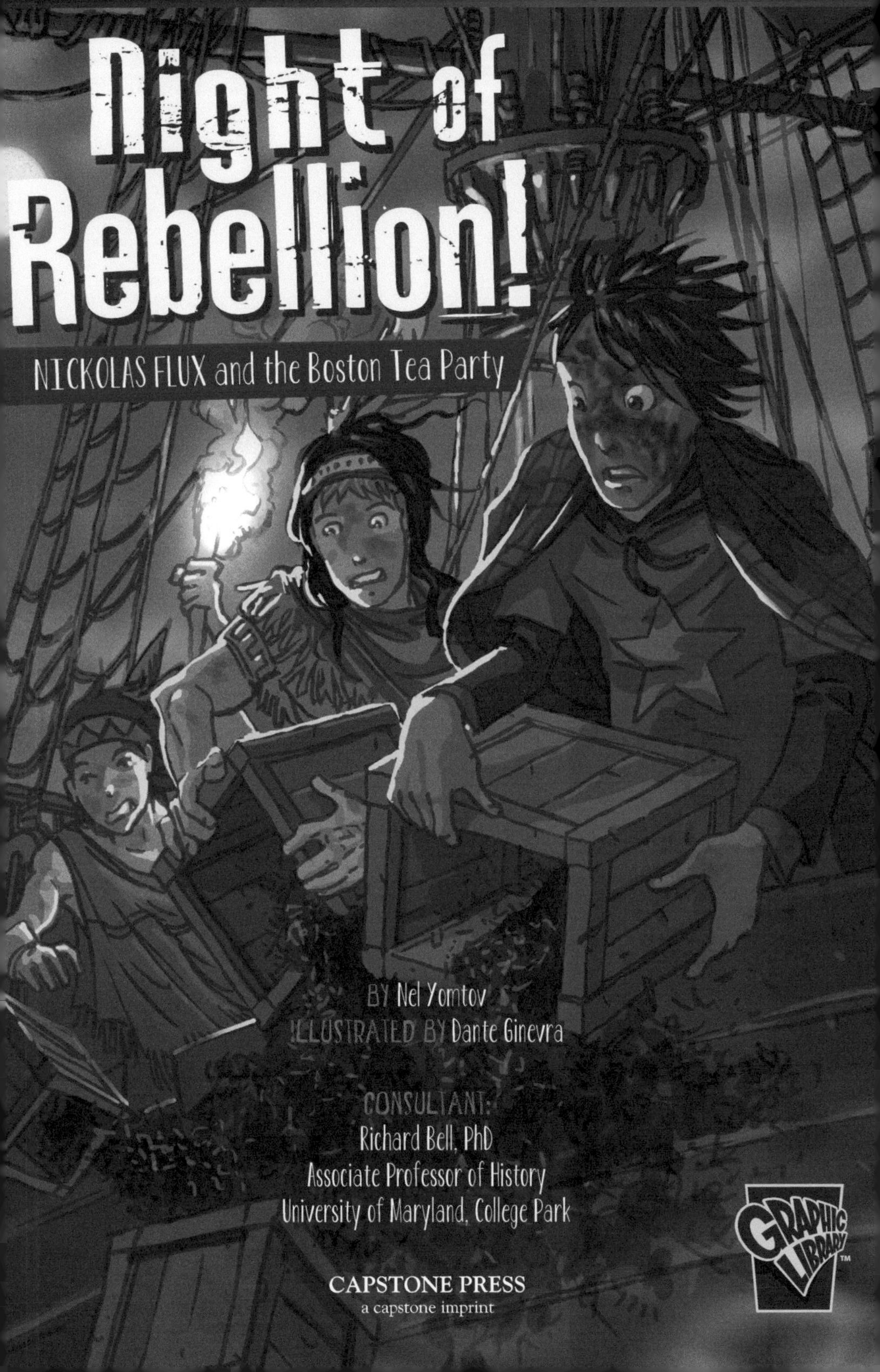

Night of Rebellion!

NICKOLAS FLUX and the Boston Tea Party

BY Nel Yomtov
ILLUSTRATED BY Dante Ginevra

CONSULTANT:
Richard Bell, PhD
Associate Professor of History
University of Maryland, College Park

GRAPHIC LIBRARY™

CAPSTONE PRESS
a capstone imprint

Graphic Library is published by Capstone Press,
1710 Roe Crest Drive, North Mankato, Minnesota 56003
www.capstonepub.com

Copyright © 2014 by Capstone Press, a Capstone imprint. All rights
reserved. No part of this publication may be reproduced in whole or in
part, or stored in a retrieval system, or transmitted in any form or by any
means, electronic, mechanical, photocopying, recording, or otherwise,
without written permission of the publisher.

Library of Congress Cataloging-in-Publication Data
Yomtov, Nelson.
 Night of rebellion! : Nickolas Flux and the Boston Tea Party / by Nel
Yomtov ; illustrated by Dante Ginevra.
    pages cm.—(Graphic library. Nickolas Flux history chronicles)
  Summary: "In graphic novel format, follows the adventures of Nickolas
Flux as he travels back in time and must survive the Boston Tea Party"—
Provided by publisher.
  Includes bibliographical references and index.
  ISBN 978-1-4765-3946-1 (library binding)
  ISBN 978-1-4765-5150-0 (paperback)
  ISBN 978-1-4765-6007-6 (eBook PDF)
1. Boston Tea Party, Boston, Mass., 1773—Juvenile literature. 2. United
States—History—Colonial period, ca. 1600-1775—Juvenile literature.
3. Boston Tea Party, Boston, Mass., 1773—Comic books, strips, etc.
4. United States—History—Colonial period, ca. 1600-1775—Comic
books, strips, etc. I. Ginevra, Dante, 1976- illustrator. II. Title.
  E215.7.Y66 2014
  973.3'115—dc23   2013028001

Photo Credits:
Design Elements: Shutterstock (backgrounds)

Editor's note:
A direct quotation, noted in red type, appears on the following page:
Page 13, from *Samuel Adams* by James K. Hosmer (New York:
Houghton Mifflin Company, 1898).

EDITOR
Christopher L. Harbo

DESIGNER
Ashlee Suker

ART DIRECTOR
Nathan Gassman

PRODUCTION SPECIALIST
Kathy McColley

Printed in the United States   5571

TABLE OF CONTENTS

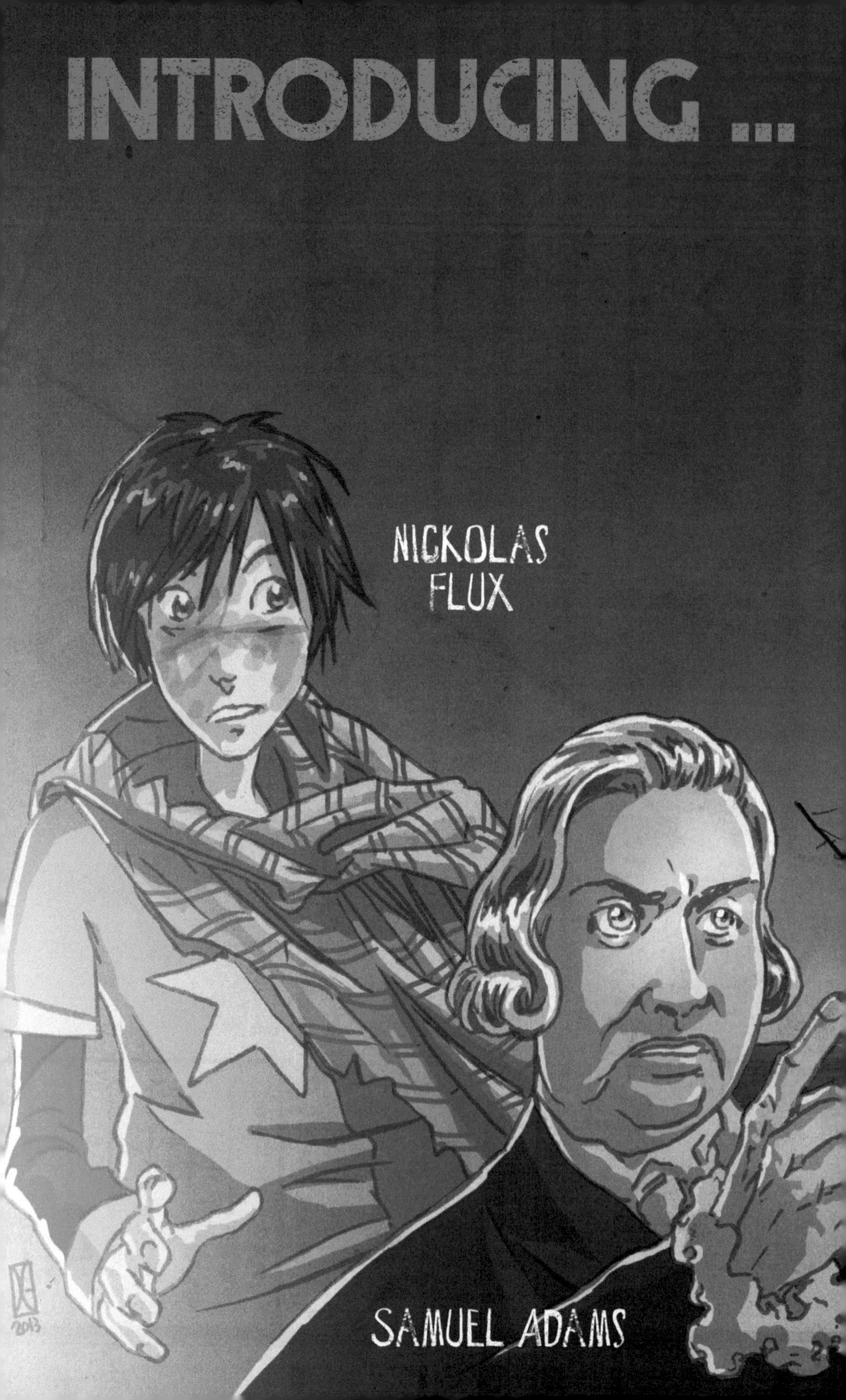
INTRODUCING ...
NICKOLAS FLUX
SAMUEL ADAMS

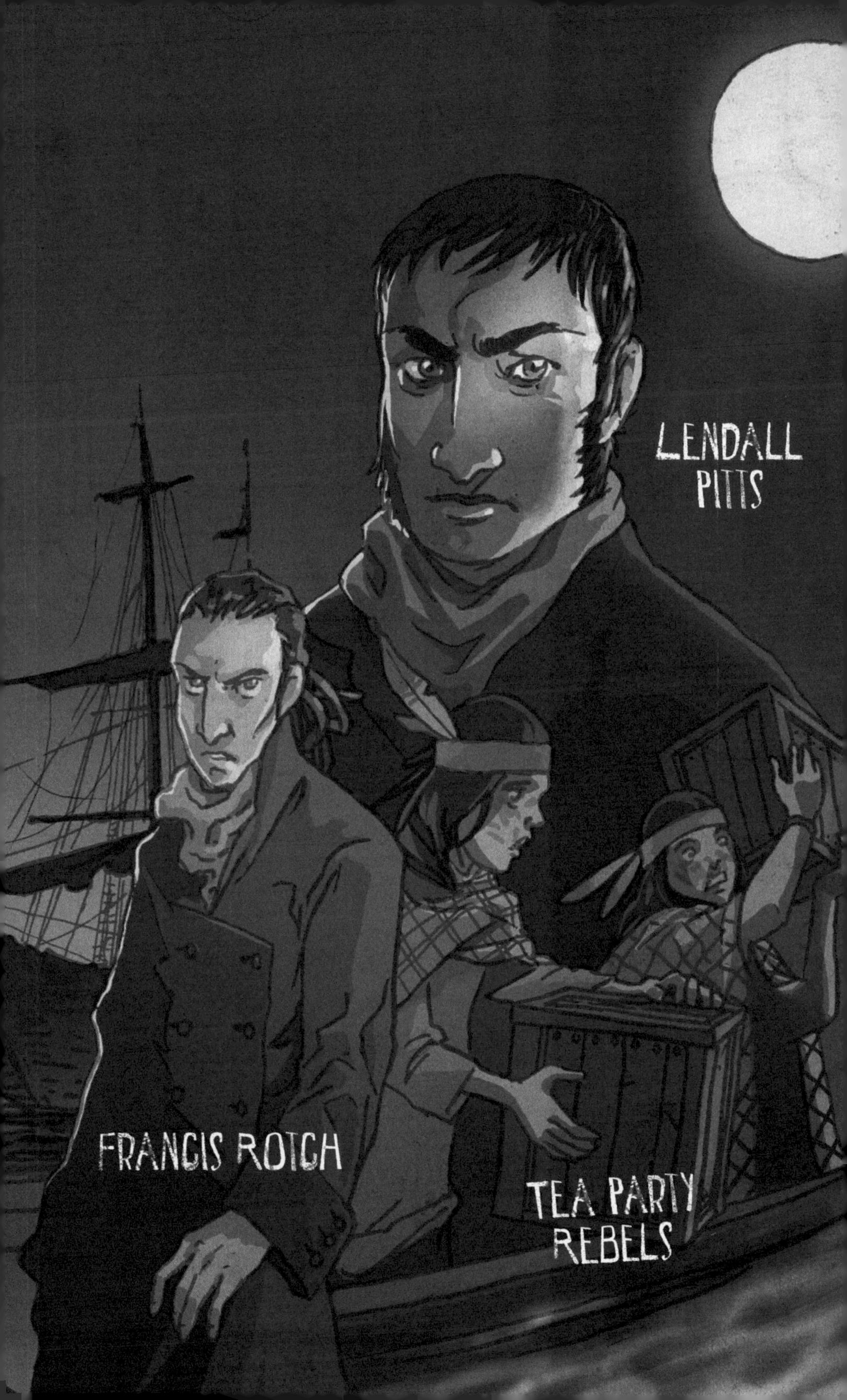
LENDALL
PITTS
FRANCIS ROTCH
TEA PARTY
REBELS

CHAPTER ONE
THE MORNING RUSH

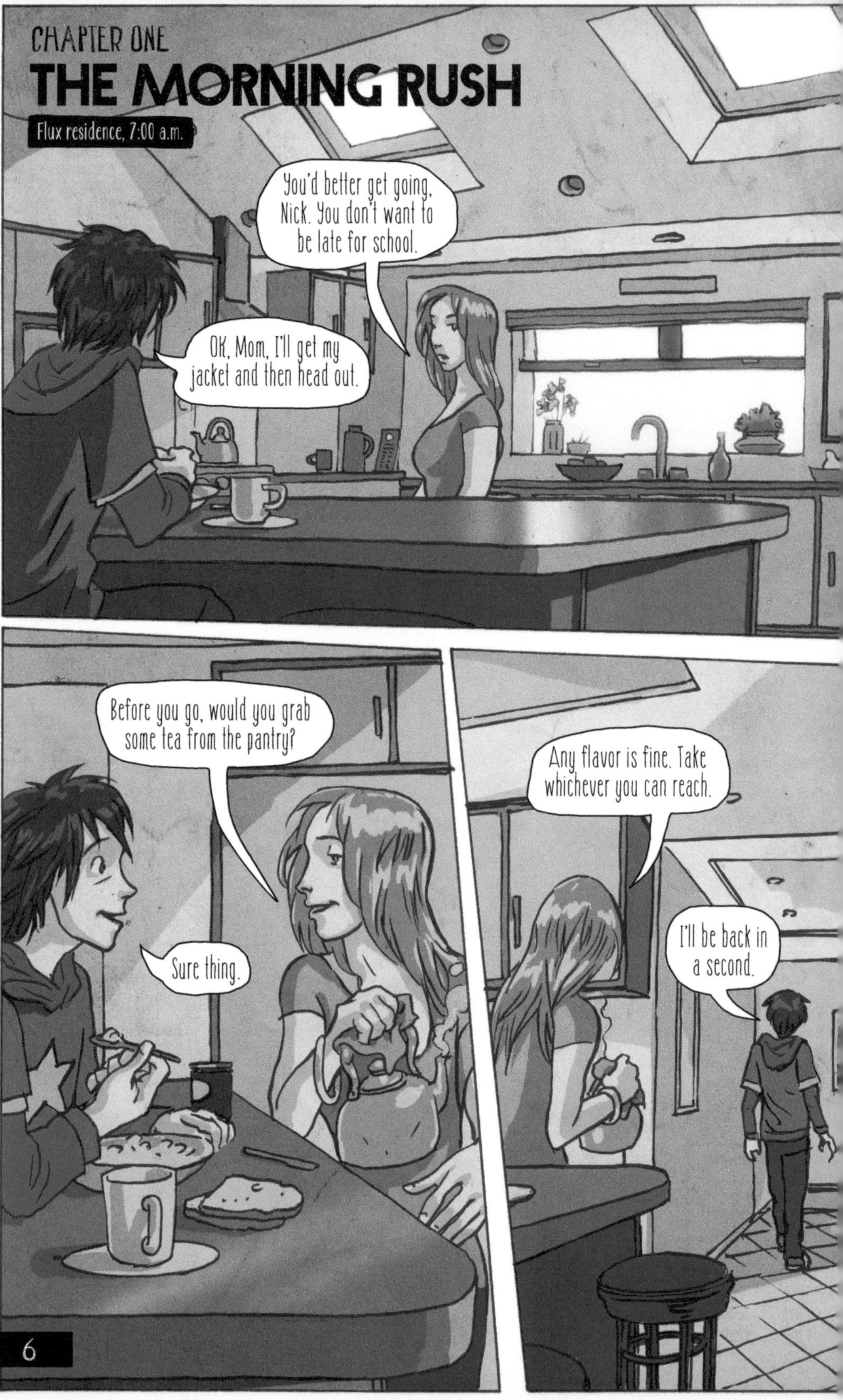
Flux residence, 7:00 a.m.
You'd better get going, Nick. You don't want to be late for school.
OK, Mom, I'll get my jacket and then head out.
Before you go, would you grab some tea from the pantry?
Sure thing.
Any flavor is fine. Take whichever you can reach.
I'll be back in a second.

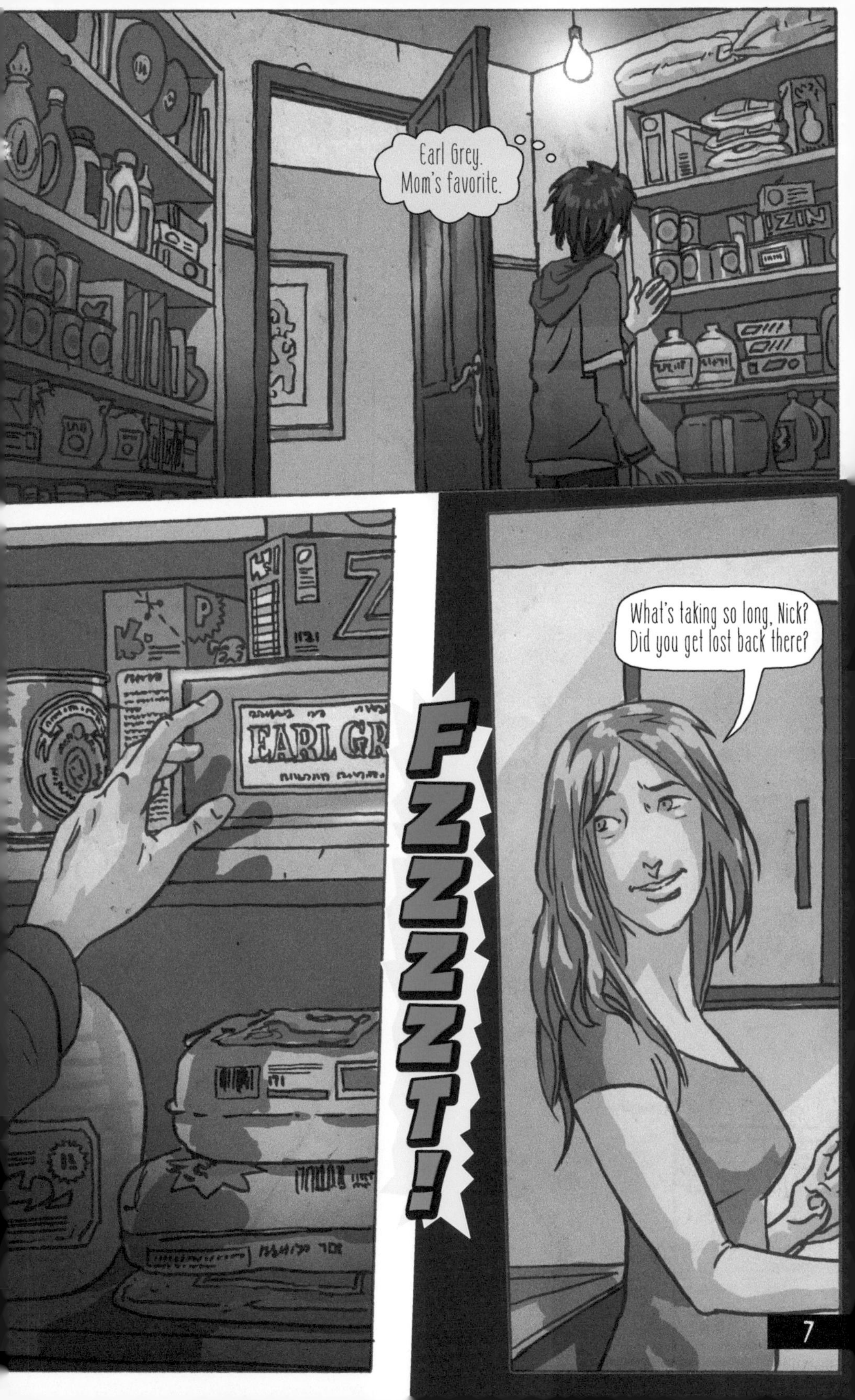
Earl Grey.
Mom's favorite.
EARL GR
FZZZZZT!
What's taking so long, Nick?
Did you get lost back there?

CHAPTER TWO
AN ANGRY MOB

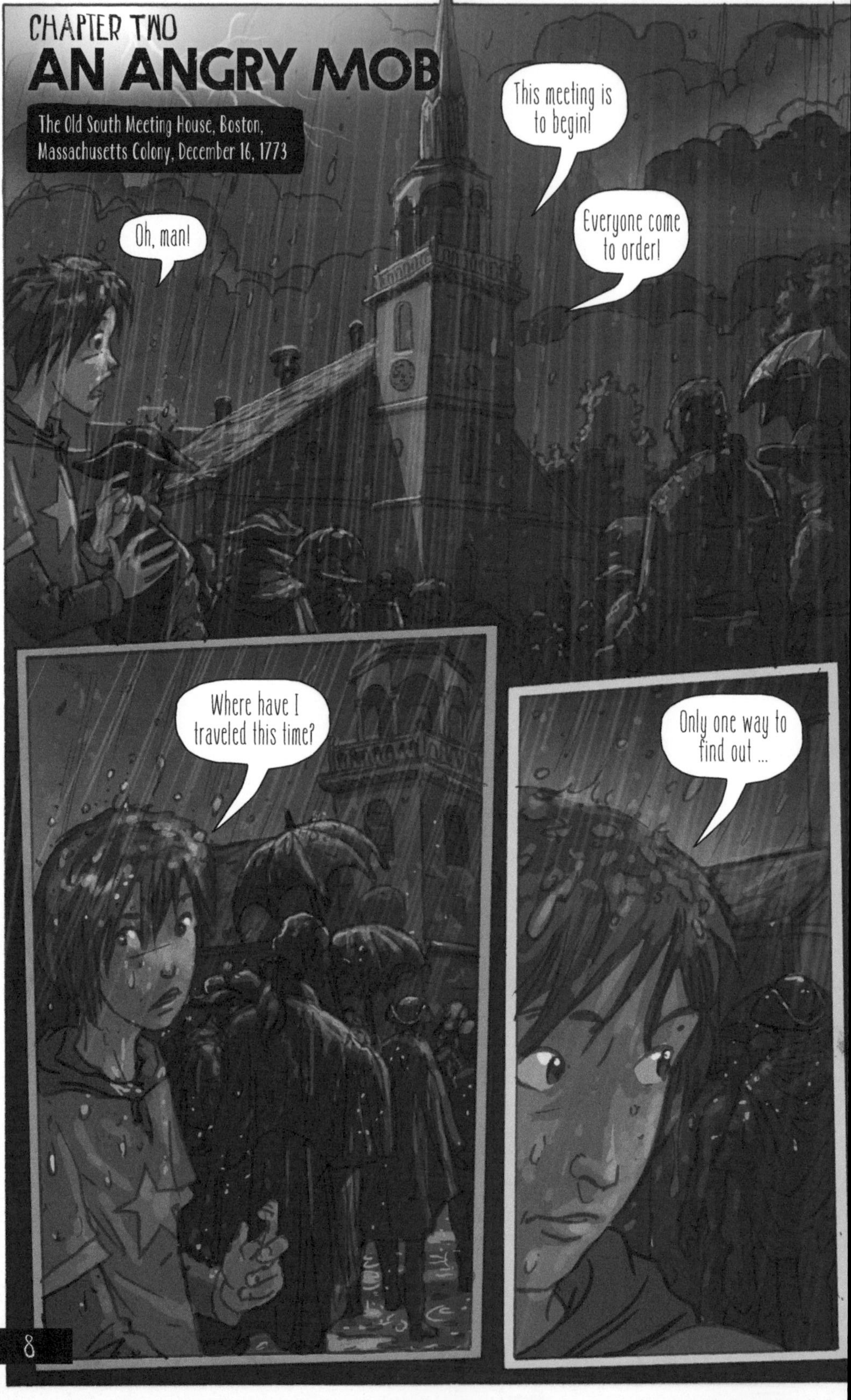

The Old South Meeting House, Boston, Massachusetts Colony, December 16, 1773
Oh, man!
This meeting is to begin!
Everyone come to order!
Where have I traveled this time?
Only one way to find out ...

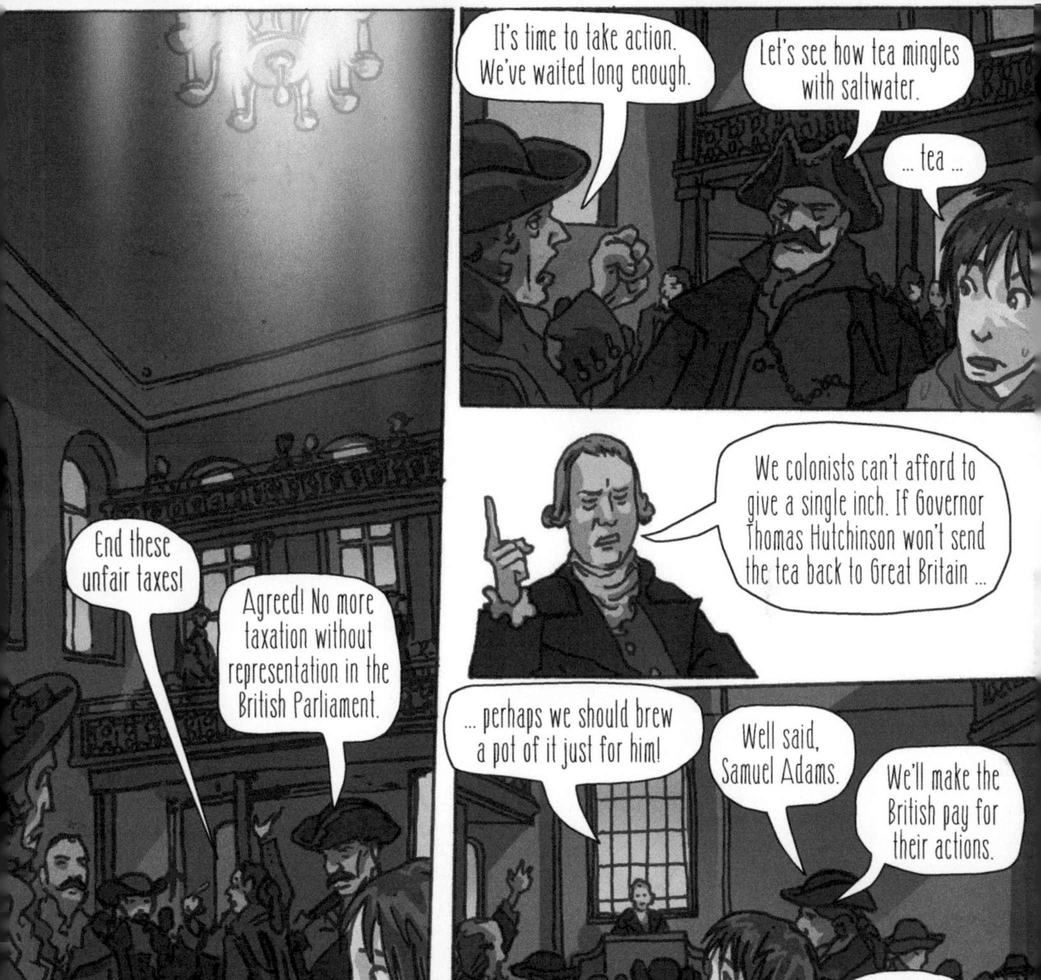
End these unfair taxes!
Agreed! No more taxation without representation in the British Parliament.
Taxation without representation ...
It's time to take action. We've waited long enough.
Let's see how tea mingles with saltwater.
... tea ...
We colonists can't afford to give a single inch. If Governor Thomas Hutchinson won't send the tea back to Great Britain ...
... perhaps we should brew a pot of it just for him!
Well said, Samuel Adams.
We'll make the British pay for their actions.
... and Samuel Adams. There's only one place I could be.
These men are preparing for the Boston Tea Party!

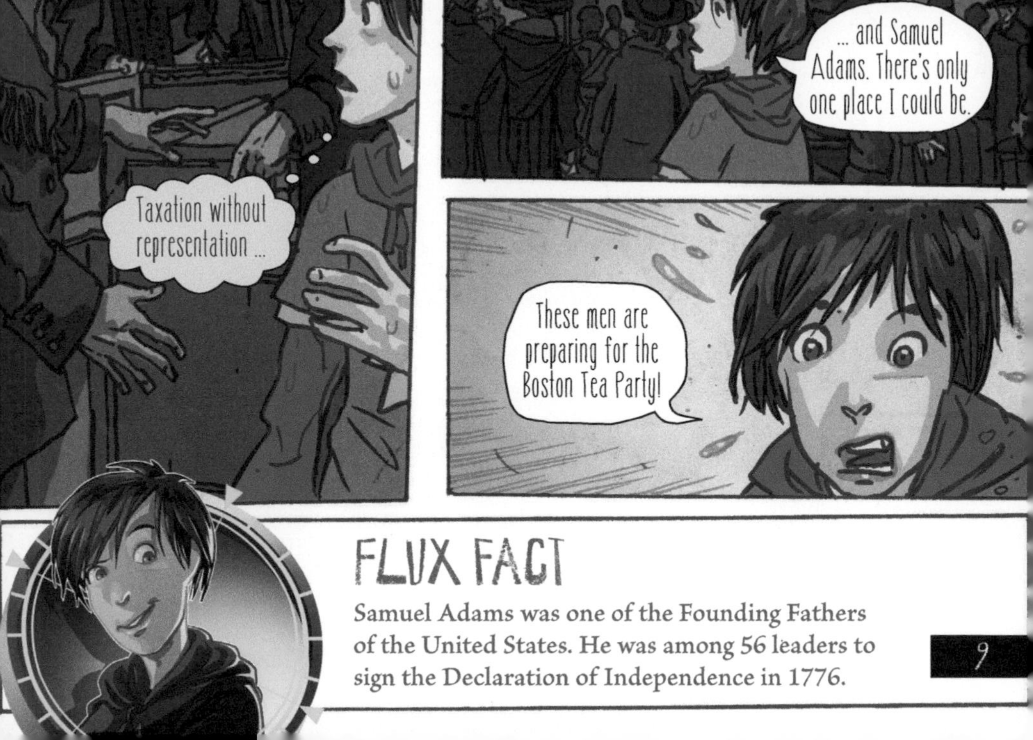

FLUX FACT

Samuel Adams was one of the Founding Fathers of the United States. He was among 56 leaders to sign the Declaration of Independence in 1776.

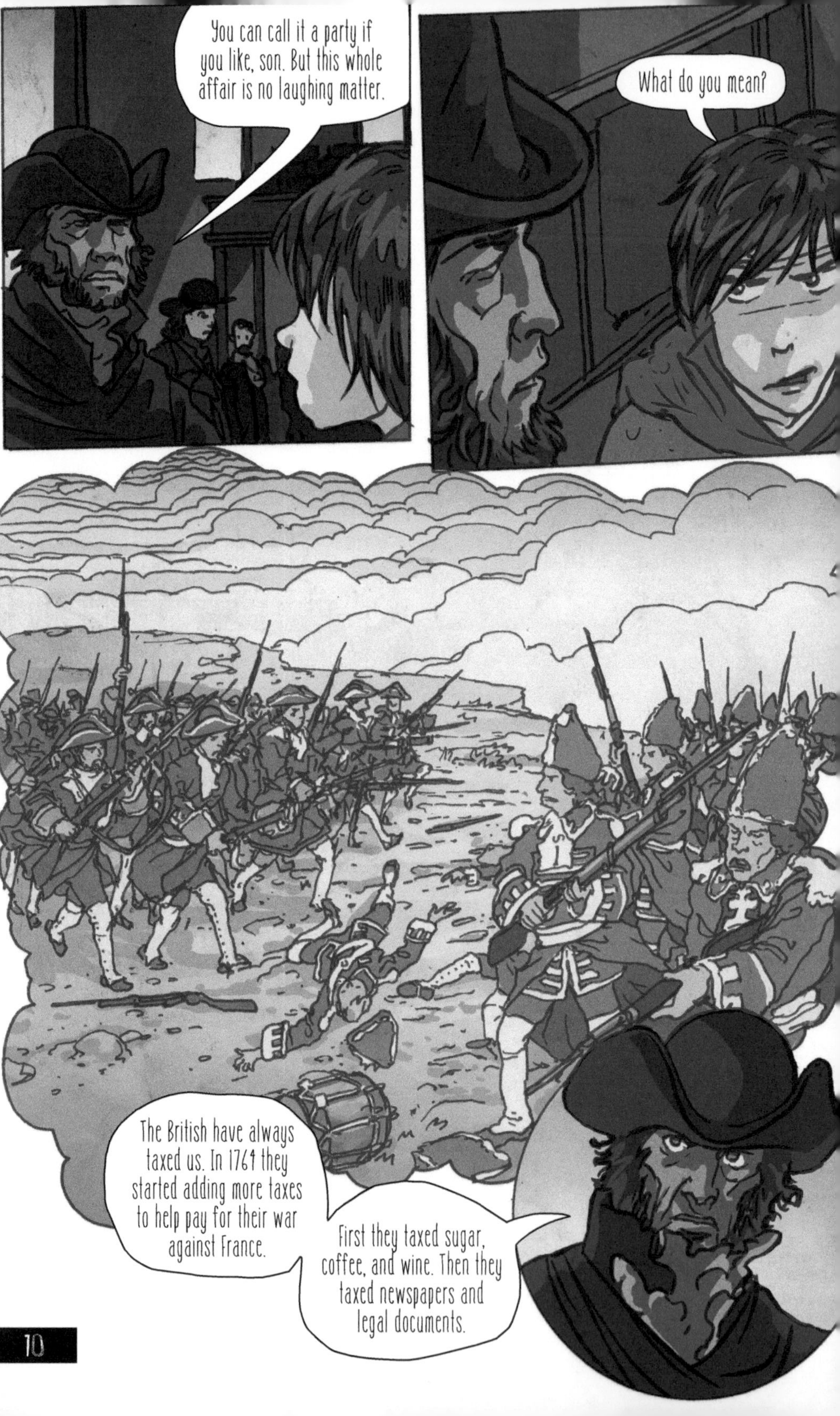
You can call it a party if you like, son. But this whole affair is no laughing matter.
What do you mean?
The British have always taxed us. In 1764 they started adding more taxes to help pay for their war against France.
First they taxed sugar, coffee, and wine. Then they taxed newspapers and legal documents.

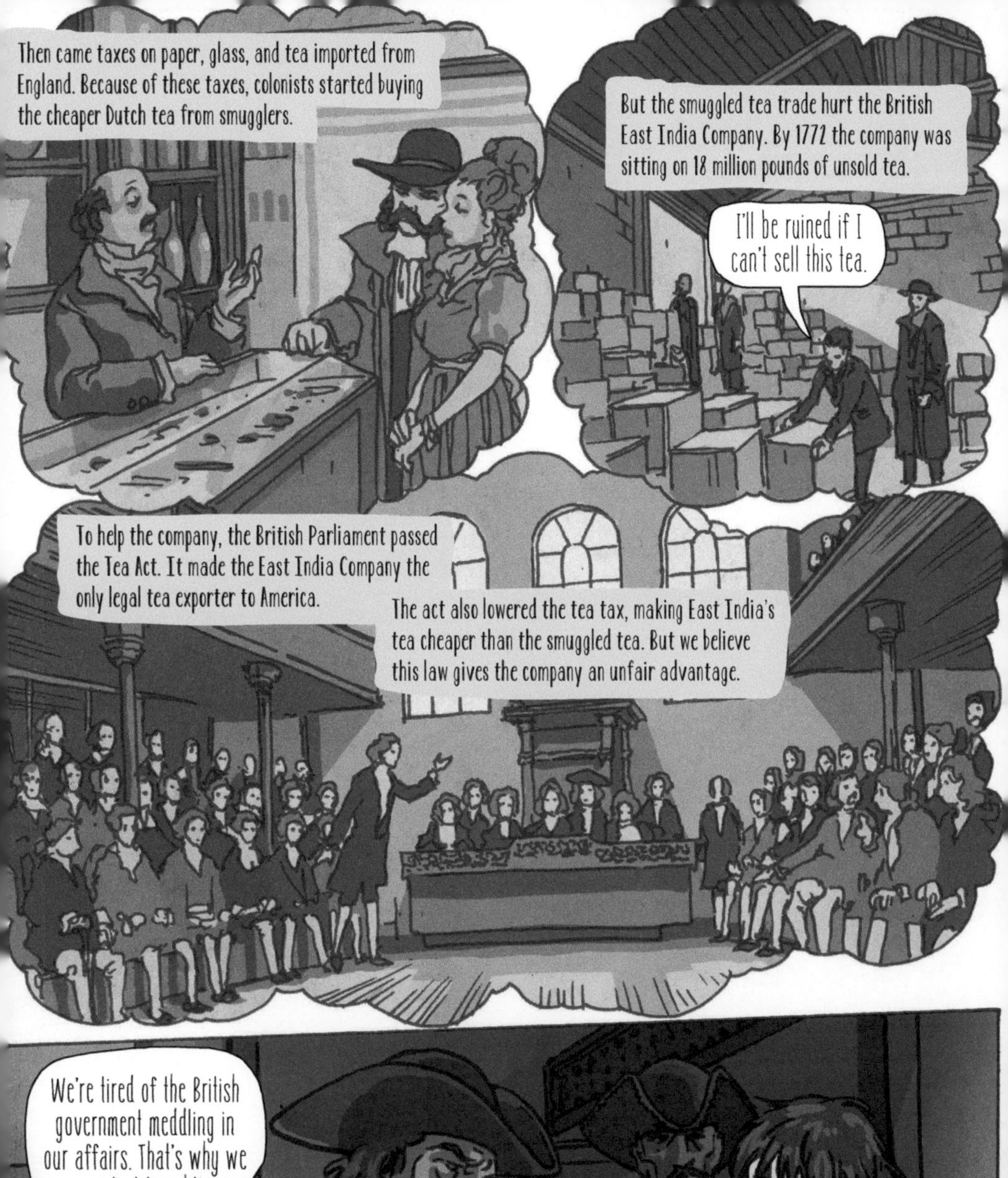
Then came taxes on paper, glass, and tea imported from England. Because of these taxes, colonists started buying the cheaper Dutch tea from smugglers.
But the smuggled tea trade hurt the British East India Company. By 1772 the company was sitting on 18 million pounds of unsold tea.
I'll be ruined if I can't sell this tea.
To help the company, the British Parliament passed the Tea Act. It made the East India Company the only legal tea exporter to America.
The act also lowered the tea tax, making East India's tea cheaper than the smuggled tea. But we believe this law gives the company an unfair advantage.
We're tired of the British government meddling in our affairs. That's why we protest tonight!

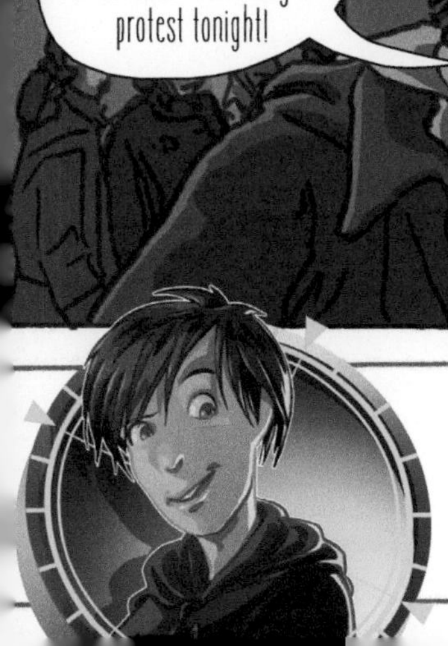

FLUX FACT

The Tea Act of 1773 also included a tax that raised money to pay the salaries of British officials in the colonies.

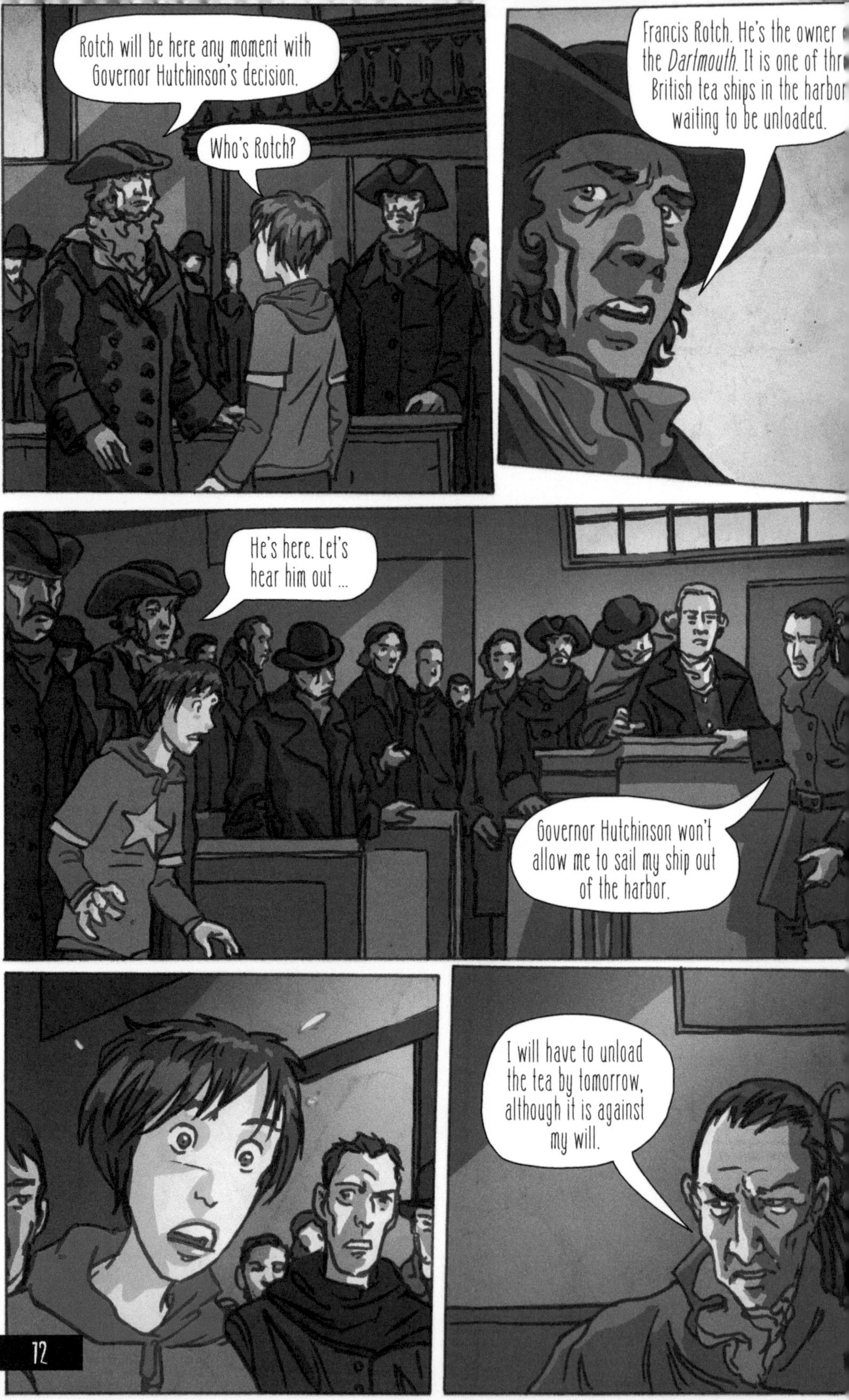
Rotch will be here any moment with Governor Hutchinson's decision.
Who's Rotch?
Francis Rotch. He's the owner the *Dartmouth*. It is one of thr British tea ships in the harbor waiting to be unloaded.
He's here. Let's hear him out ...
Governor Hutchinson won't allow me to sail my ship out of the harbor.
I will have to unload the tea by tomorrow, although it is against my will.

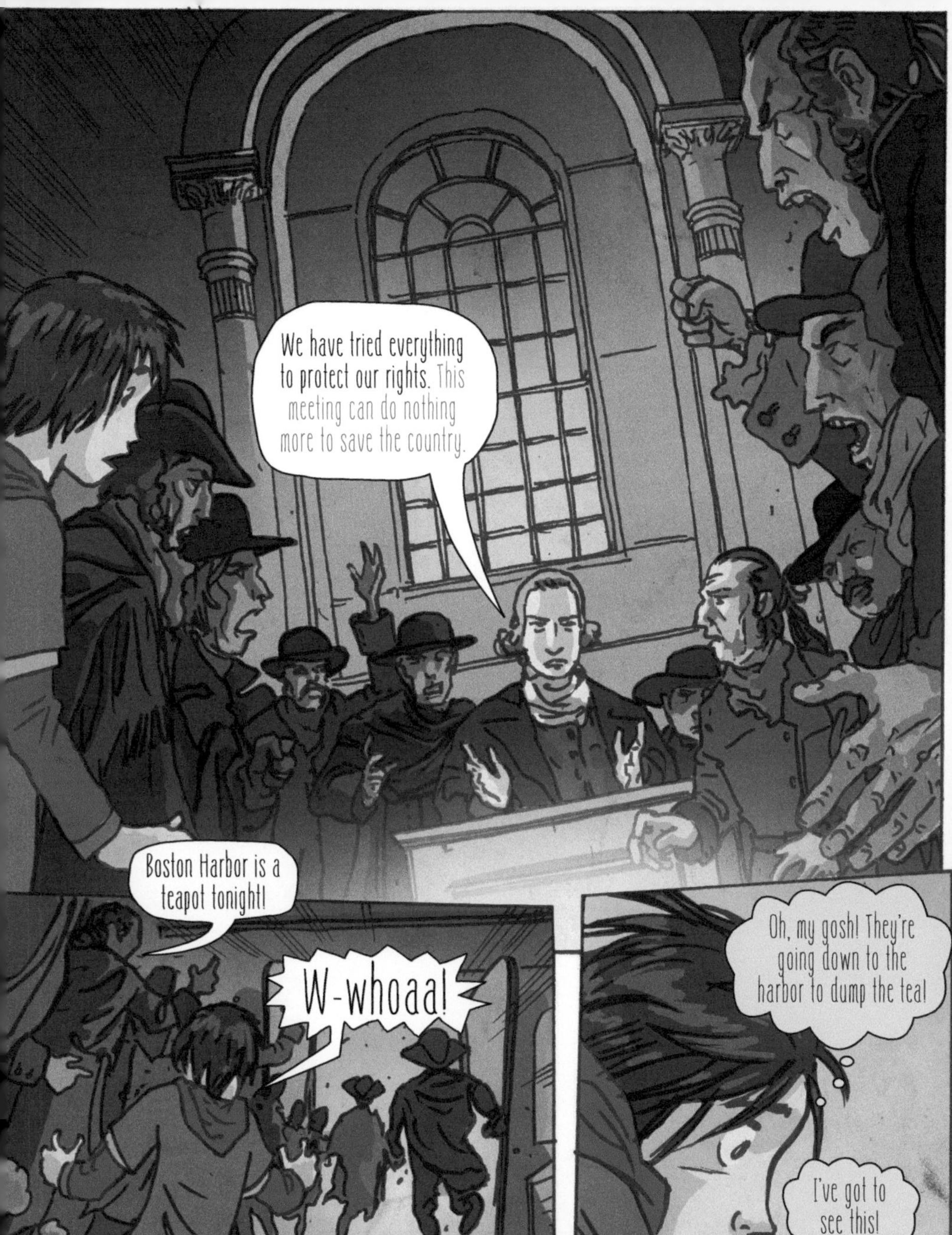
We have tried everything to protect our rights. This meeting can do nothing more to save the country.
Boston Harbor is a teapot tonight!
W-whoaa!
Oh, my gosh! They're going down to the harbor to dump the tea!
I've got to see this!

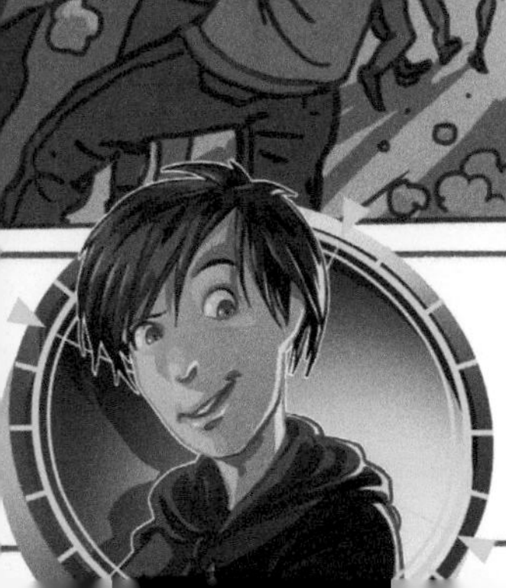

FLUX FACT

About 5,000 people attended the meeting at the Old South Meeting House. Some historians believe Adams' quotation above was a signal to dump the tea.

CHAPTER THREE

AN ACT OF TREASON

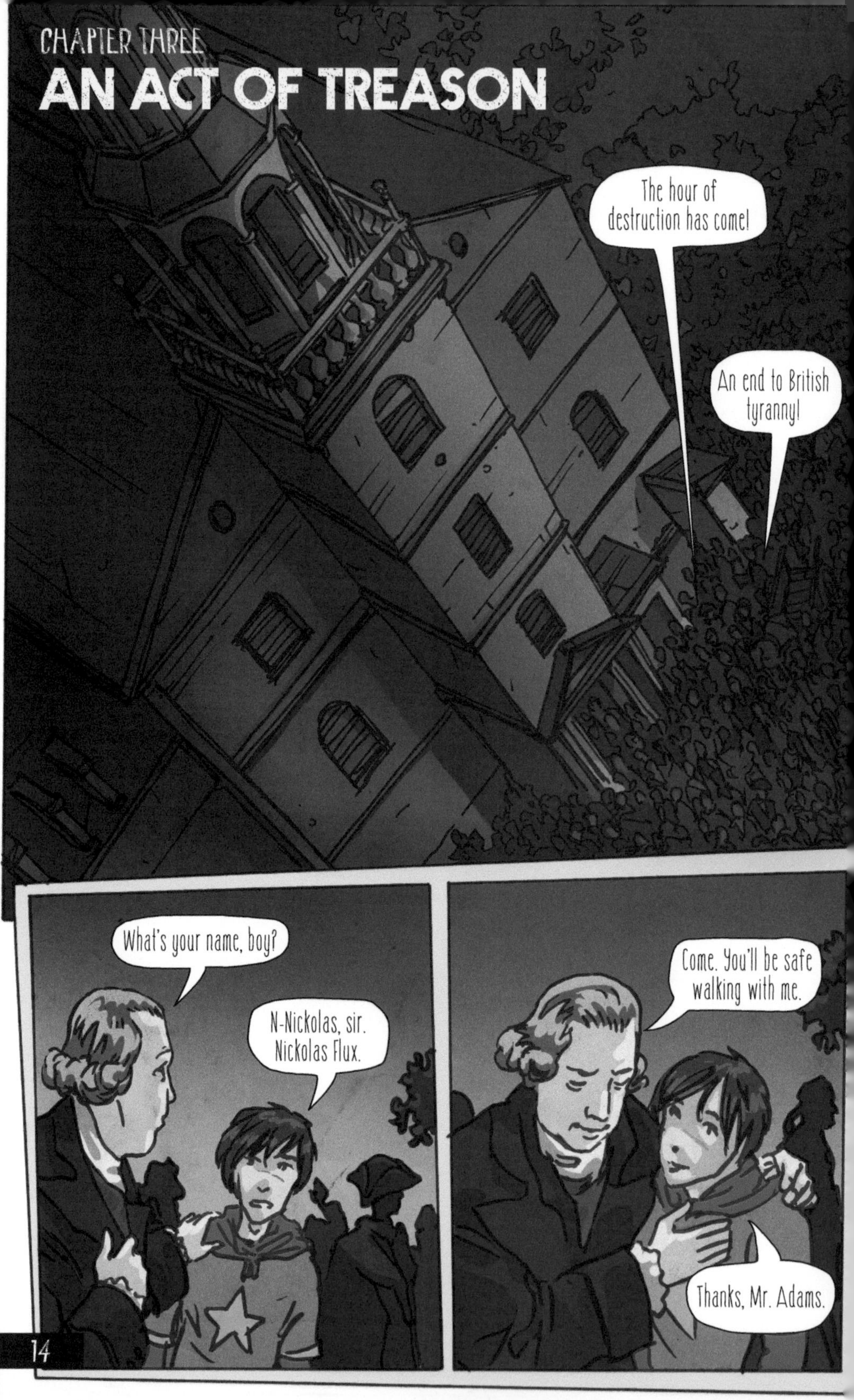
The hour of destruction has come!
An end to British tyranny!
What's your name, boy?
N-Nickolas, sir. Nickolas Flux.
Come. You'll be safe walking with me.
Thanks, Mr. Adams.

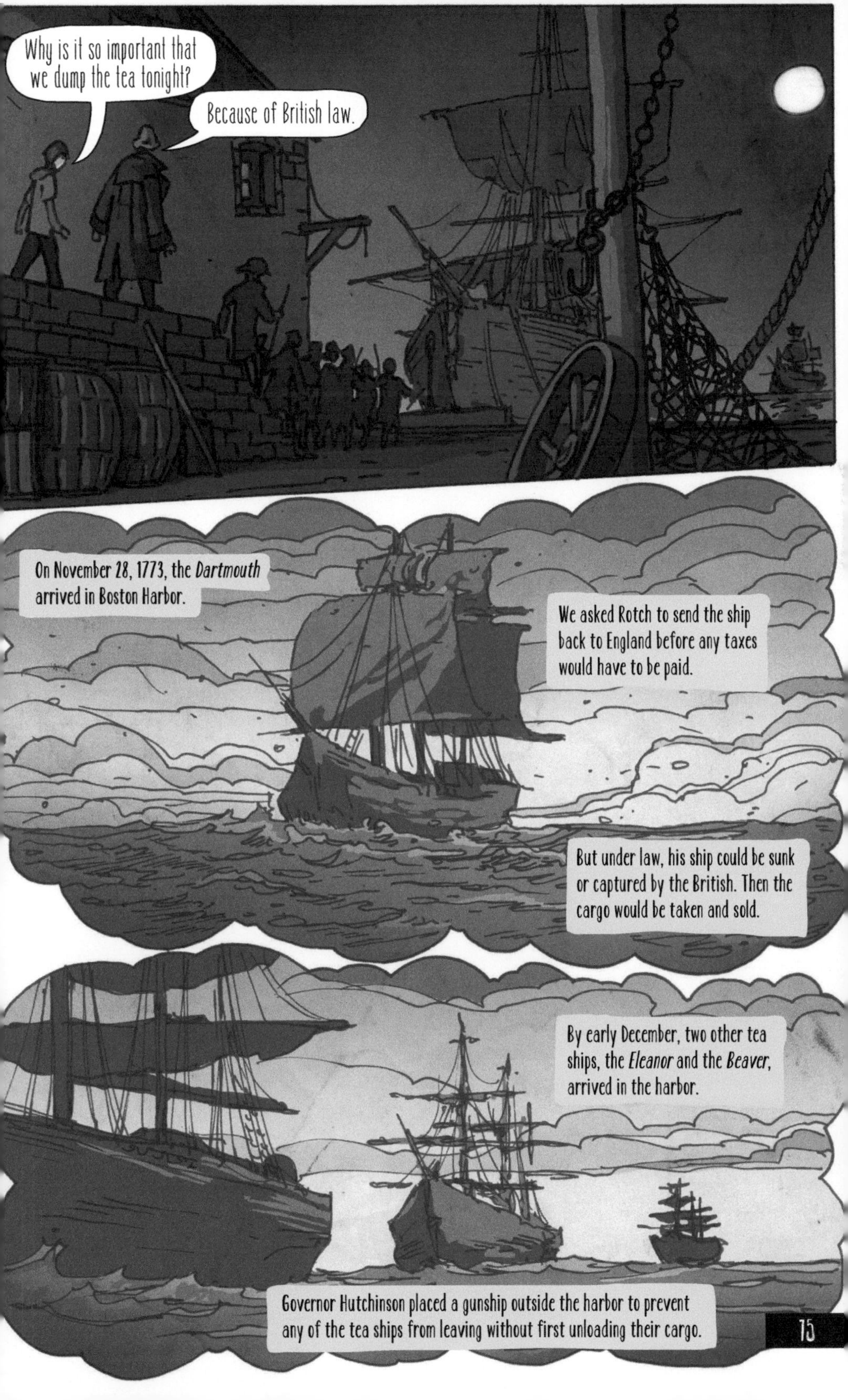
Why is it so important that we dump the tea tonight?
Because of British law.
On November 28, 1773, the *Dartmouth* arrived in Boston Harbor.
We asked Rotch to send the ship back to England before any taxes would have to be paid.
But under law, his ship could be sunk or captured by the British. Then the cargo would be taken and sold.
By early December, two other tea ships, the *Eleanor* and the *Beaver*, arrived in the harbor.
Governor Hutchinson placed a gunship outside the harbor to prevent any of the tea ships from leaving without first unloading their cargo.

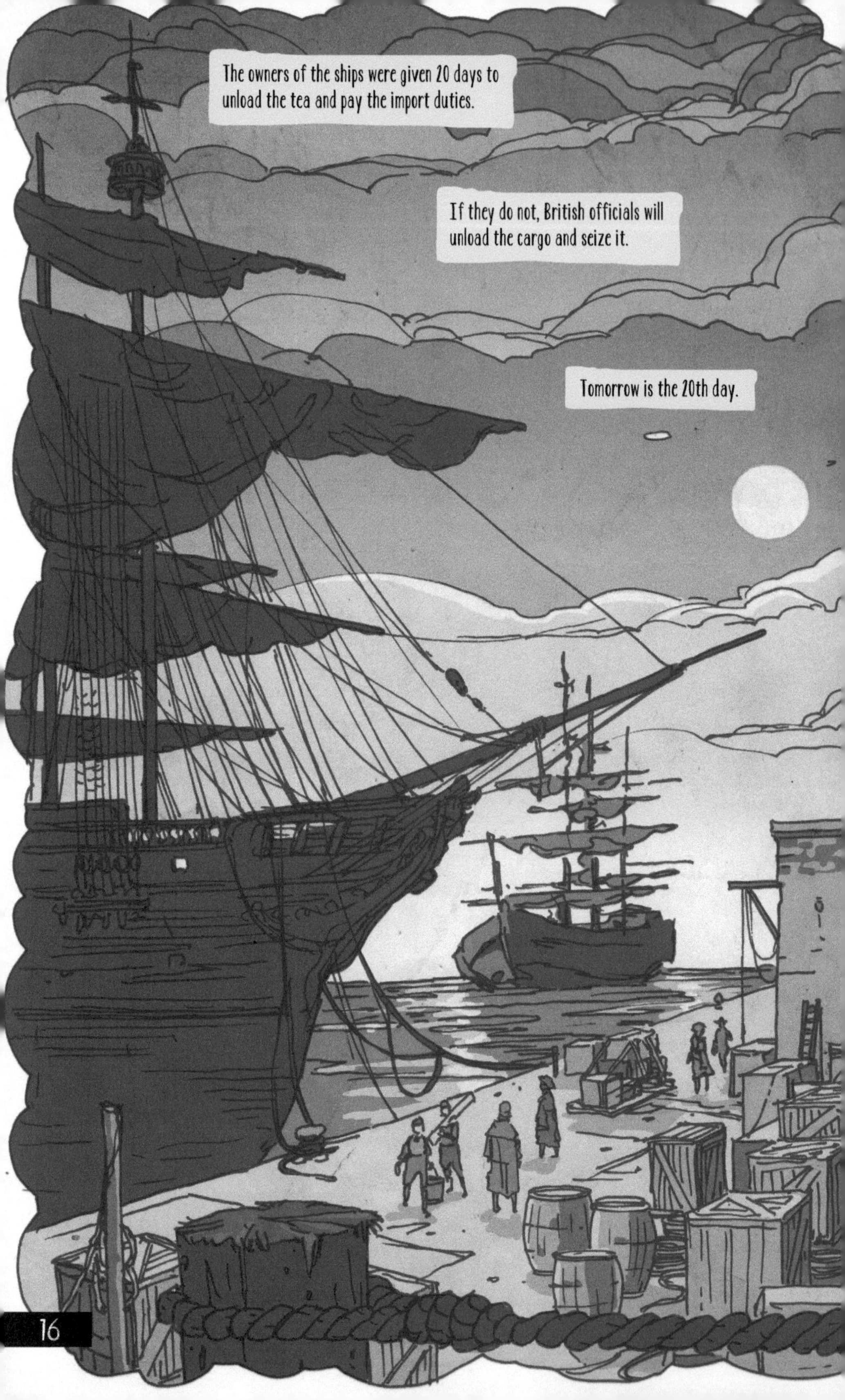
The owners of the ships were given 20 days to unload the tea and pay the import duties.
If they do not, British officials will unload the cargo and seize it.
Tomorrow is the 20th day.

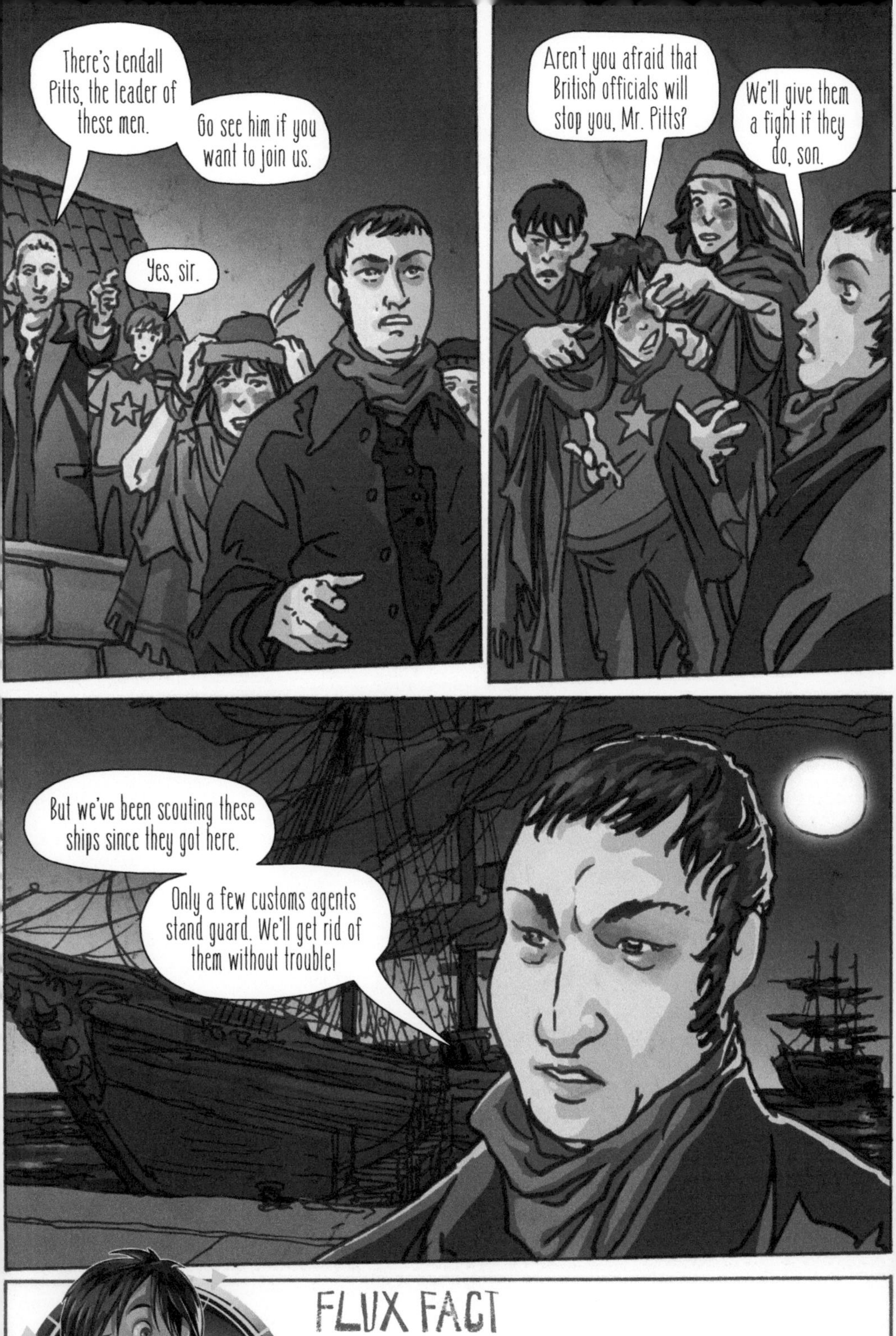
There's Lendall Pitts, the leader of these men.
Go see him if you want to join us.
Yes, sir.
Aren't you afraid that British officials will stop you, Mr. Pitts?
We'll give them a fight if they do, son.
But we've been scouting these ships since they got here.
Only a few customs agents stand guard. We'll get rid of them without trouble!

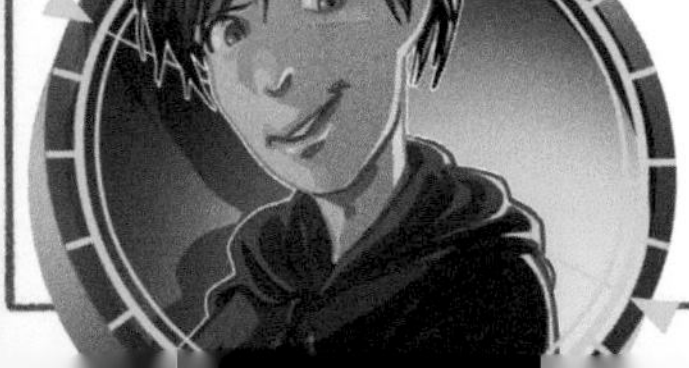

FLUX FACT

Lendall Pitts was an active member of the Sons of Liberty. American patriots formed this group to protect the colonists' rights and to protest the taxes by the British government.

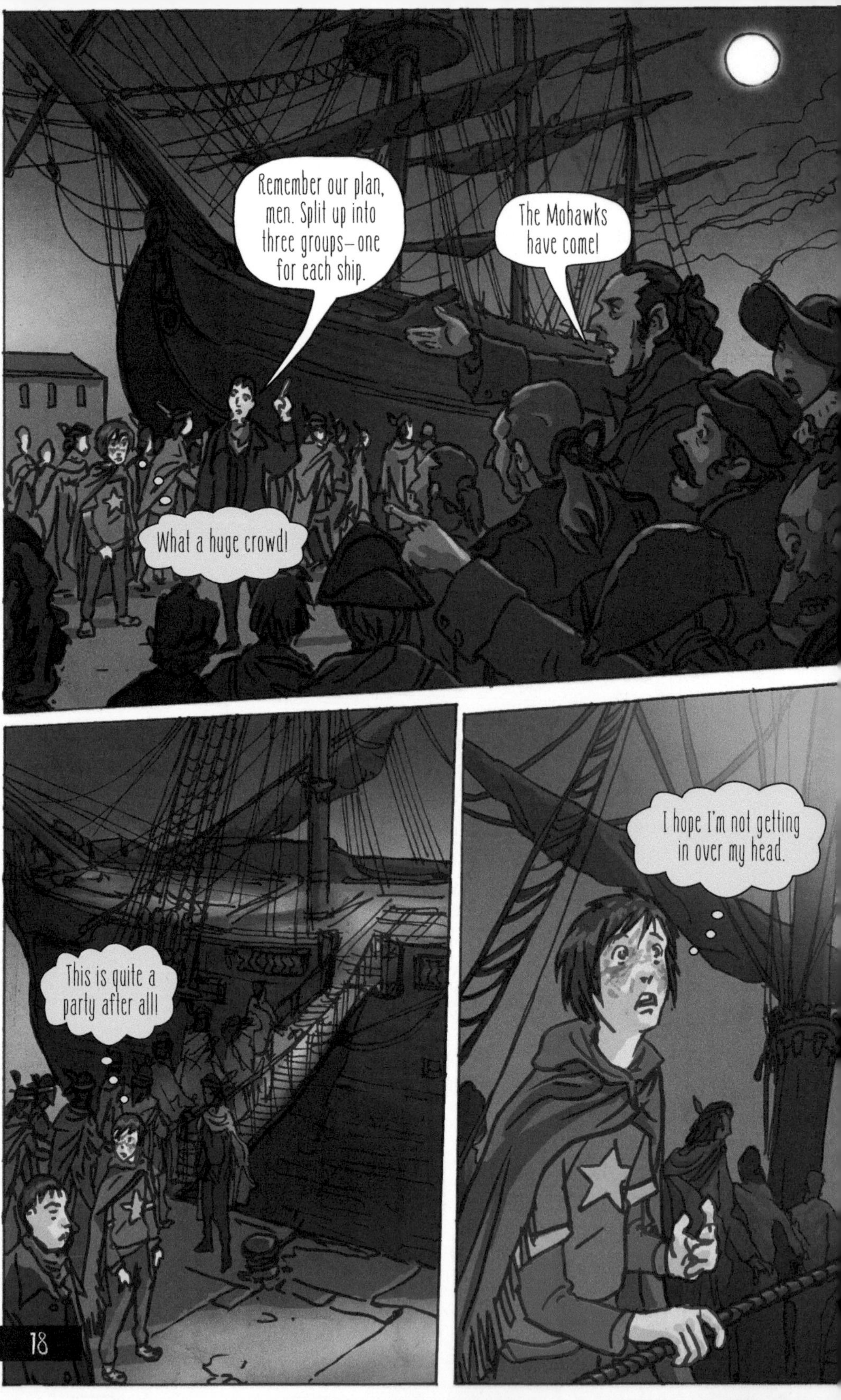
Remember our plan, men. Split up into three groups—one for each ship.
The Mohawks have come!
What a huge crowd!
This is quite a party after all!
I hope I'm not getting in over my head.

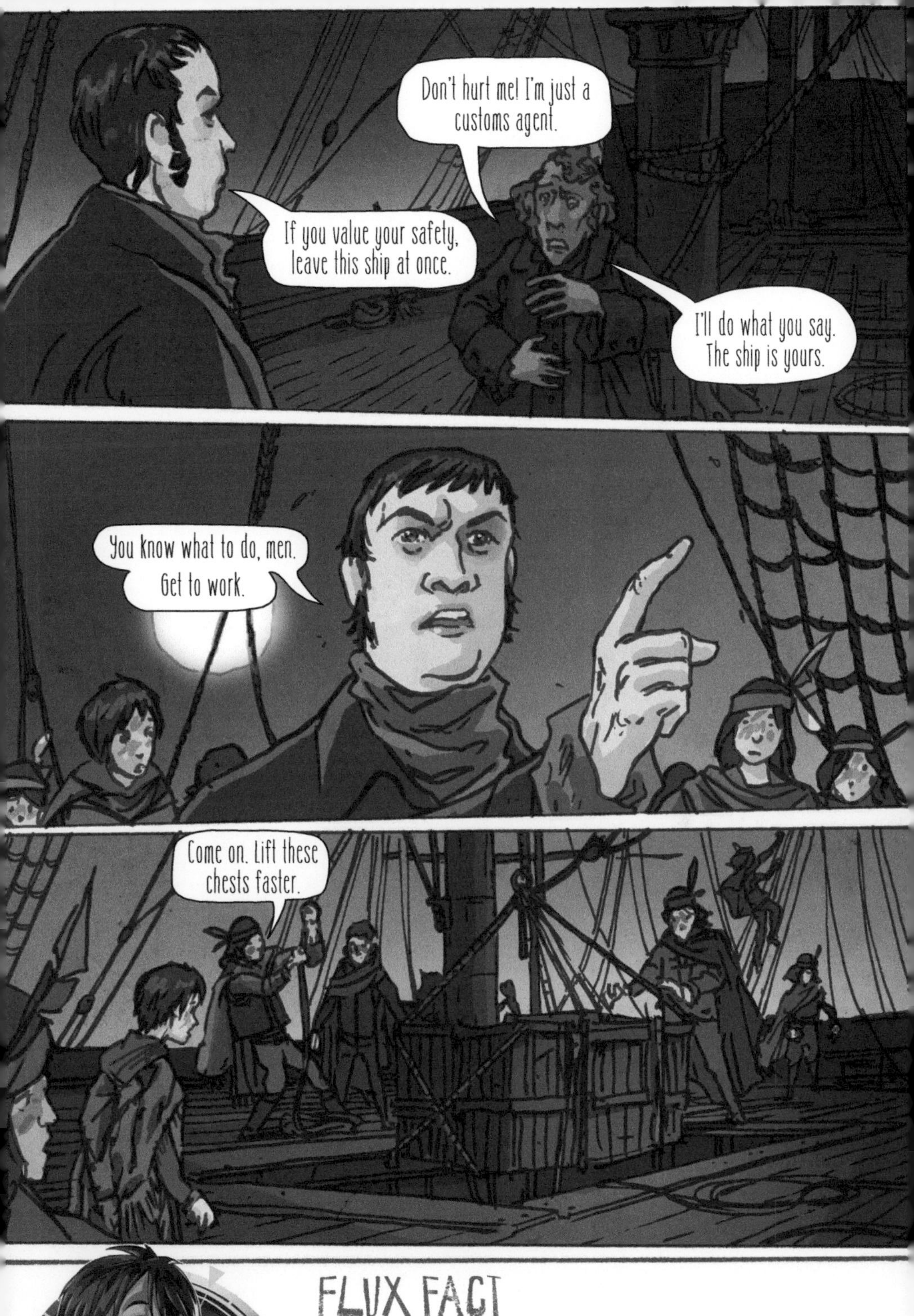
Don't hurt me! I'm just a customs agent.
If you value your safety, leave this ship at once.
I'll do what you say. The ship is yours.
You know what to do, men. Get to work.
Come on. Lift these chests faster.

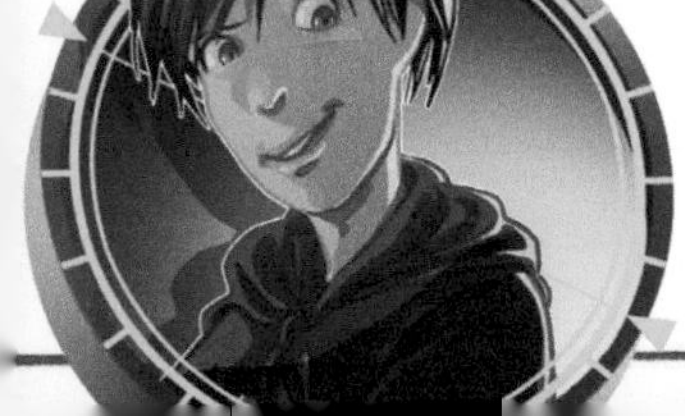

FLUX FACT

Many historians doubt that the protestors wore full Mohawk Indian dress. Firsthand reports say that most of the participants disguised themselves with ragged blankets and soot-smeared faces. Some wore feathers in their hair.

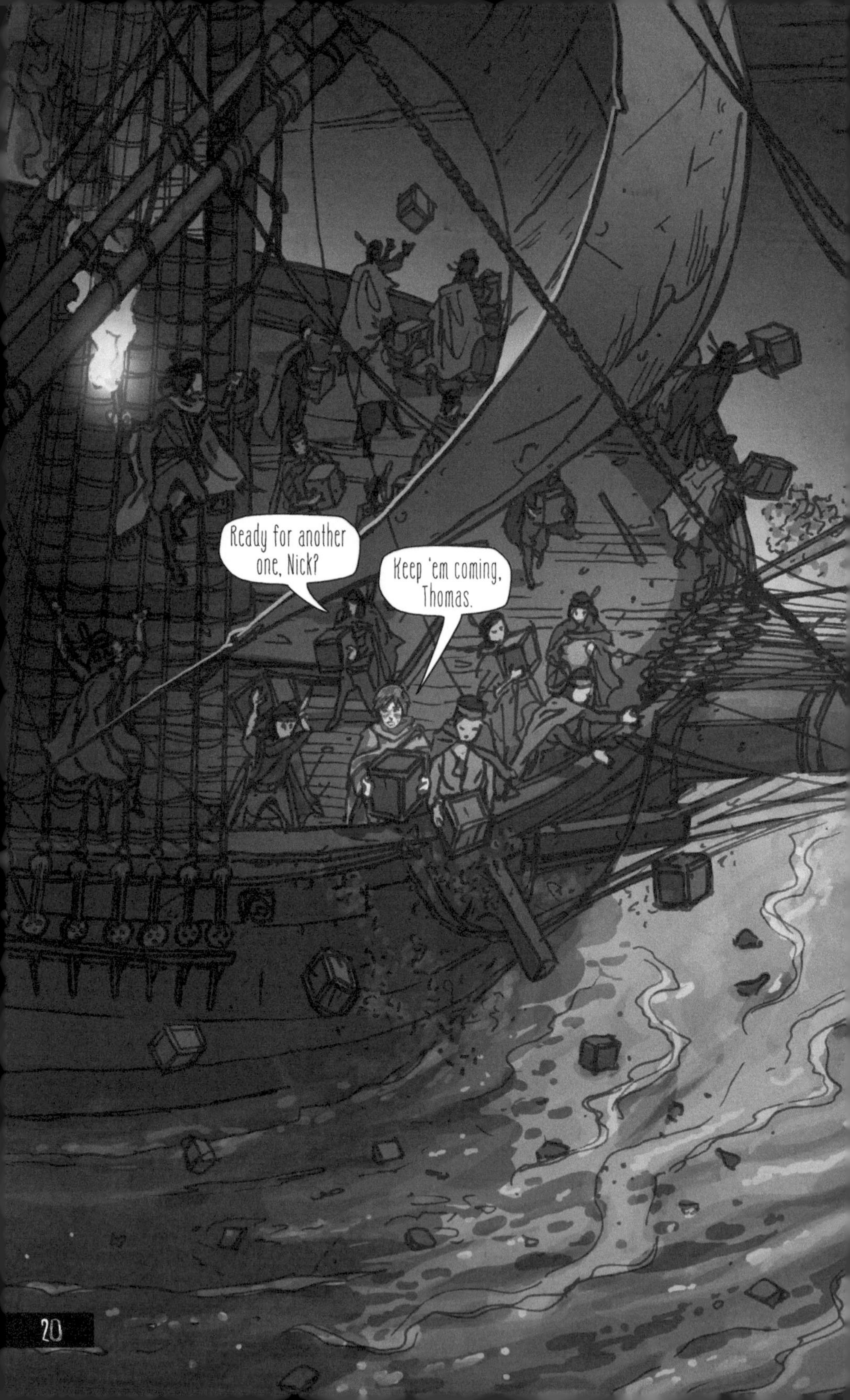
Ready for another one, Nick?
Keep 'em coming, Thomas.

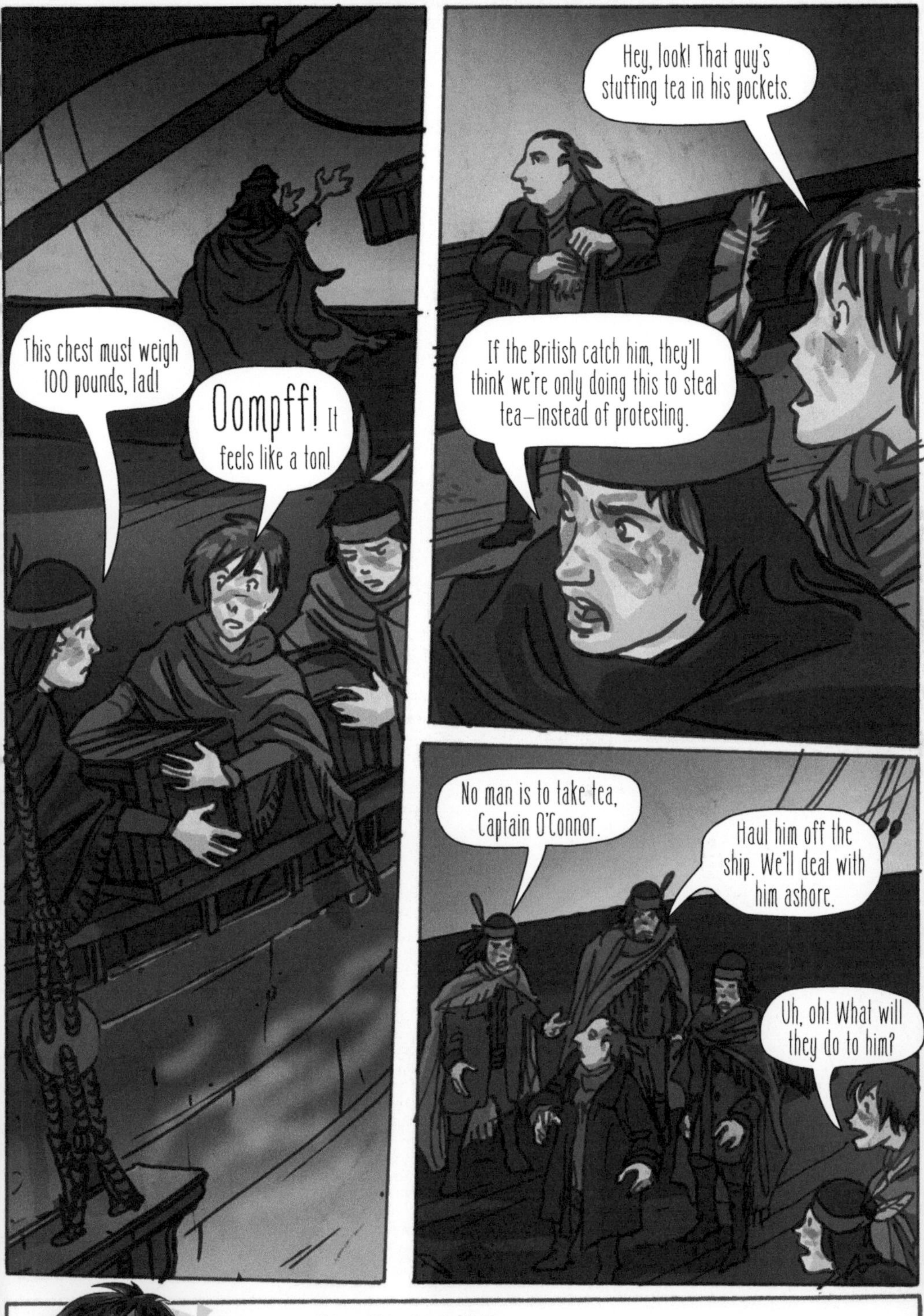
This chest must weigh 100 pounds, lad!
Oompff! It feels like a ton!
Hey, look! That guy's stuffing tea in his pockets.
If the British catch him, they'll think we're only doing this to steal tea—instead of protesting.
No man is to take tea, Captain O'Connor.
Haul him off the ship. We'll deal with him ashore.
Uh, oh! What will they do to him?

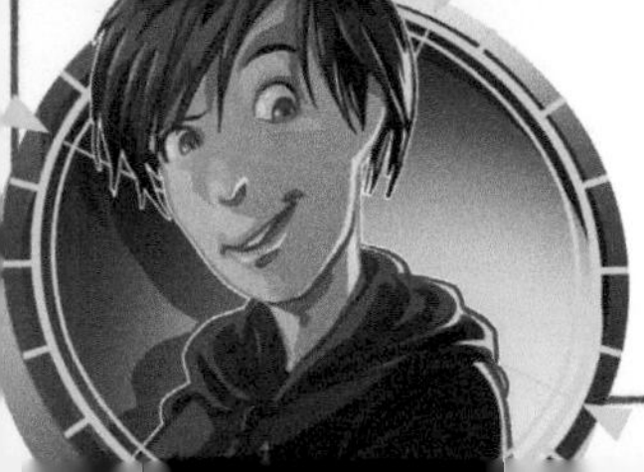

FLUX FACT

The Boston Tea Party lasted three hours. In all, 342 chests containing 90,000 pounds (41 metric tons) of tea were thrown overboard. In today's money, the cost of the tea would be equal to about $1 million.

CHAPTER FOUR
DISASTER!

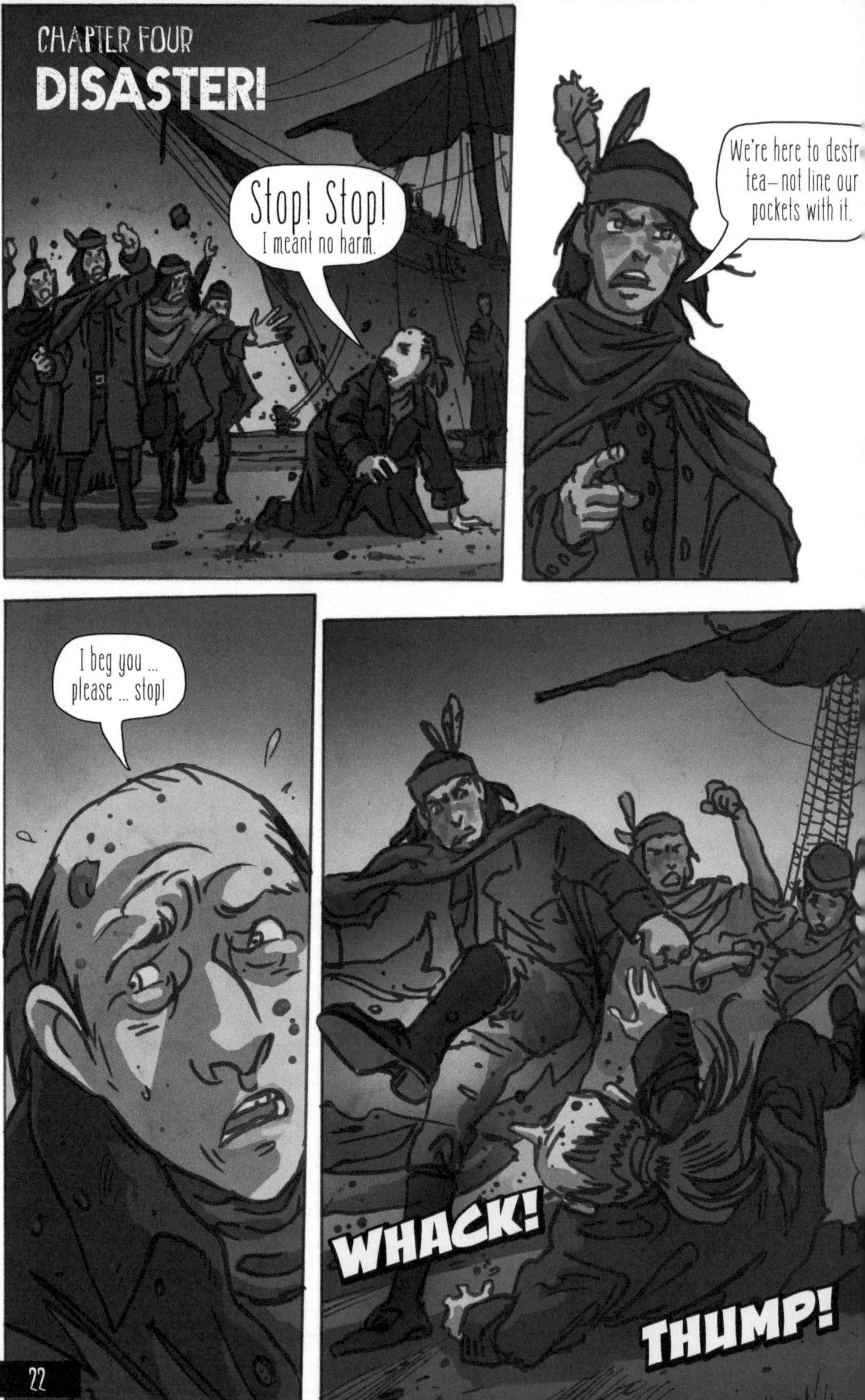
Stop! Stop!
I meant no harm.
We're here to destr
tea—not line our
pockets with it.
I beg you ... please ... stop!
WHACK!
THUMP!

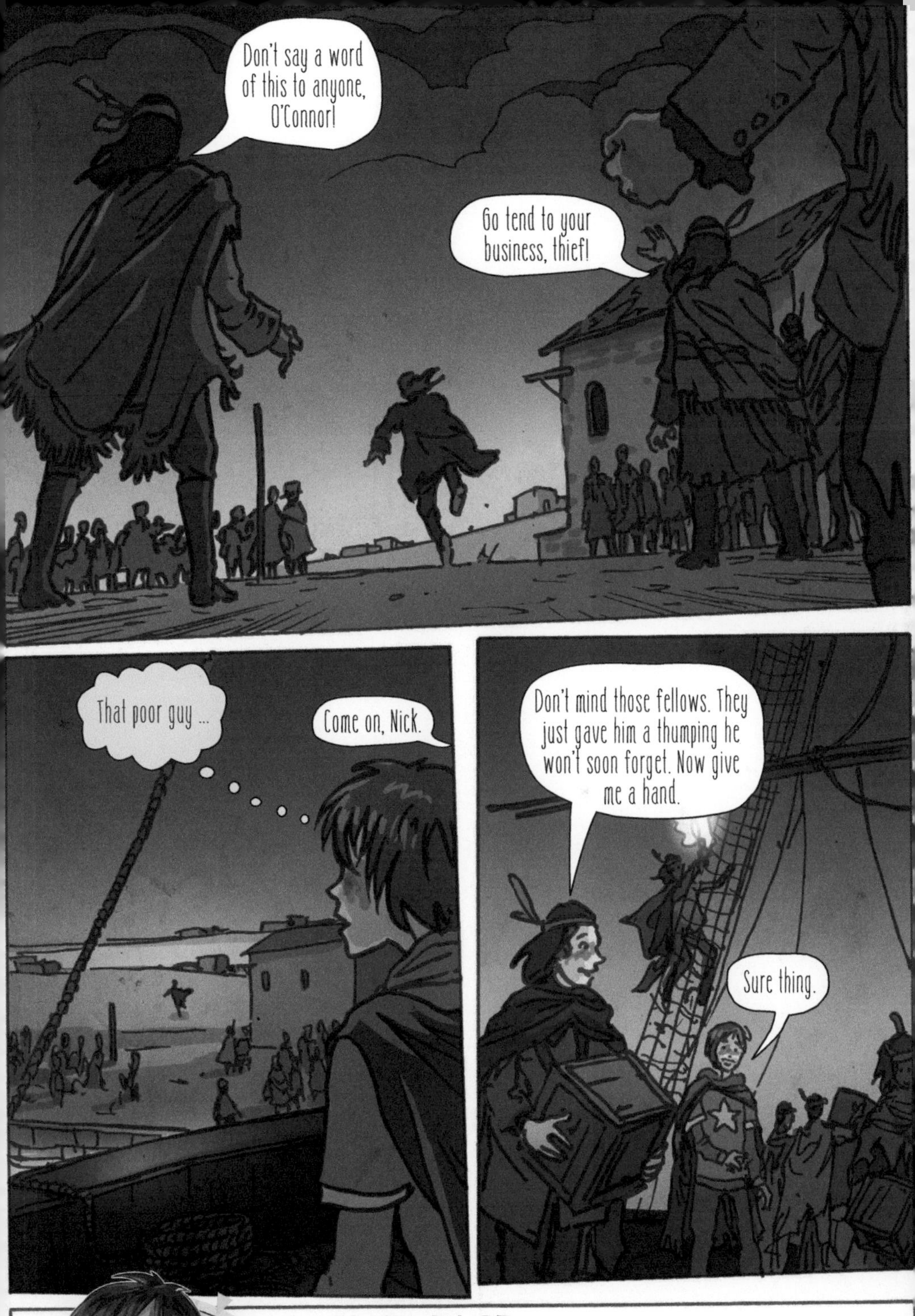

Don't say a word of this to anyone, O'Connor!
Go tend to your business, thief!
That poor guy ...
Come on, Nick.
Don't mind those fellows. They just gave him a thumping he won't soon forget. Now give me a hand.
Sure thing.

FLUX FACT

Captain Charles O'Connor owned an inn and a stable in Boston. His attempt to steal tea endangered the secrecy of the Tea Party. It made him very unpopular in Boston.

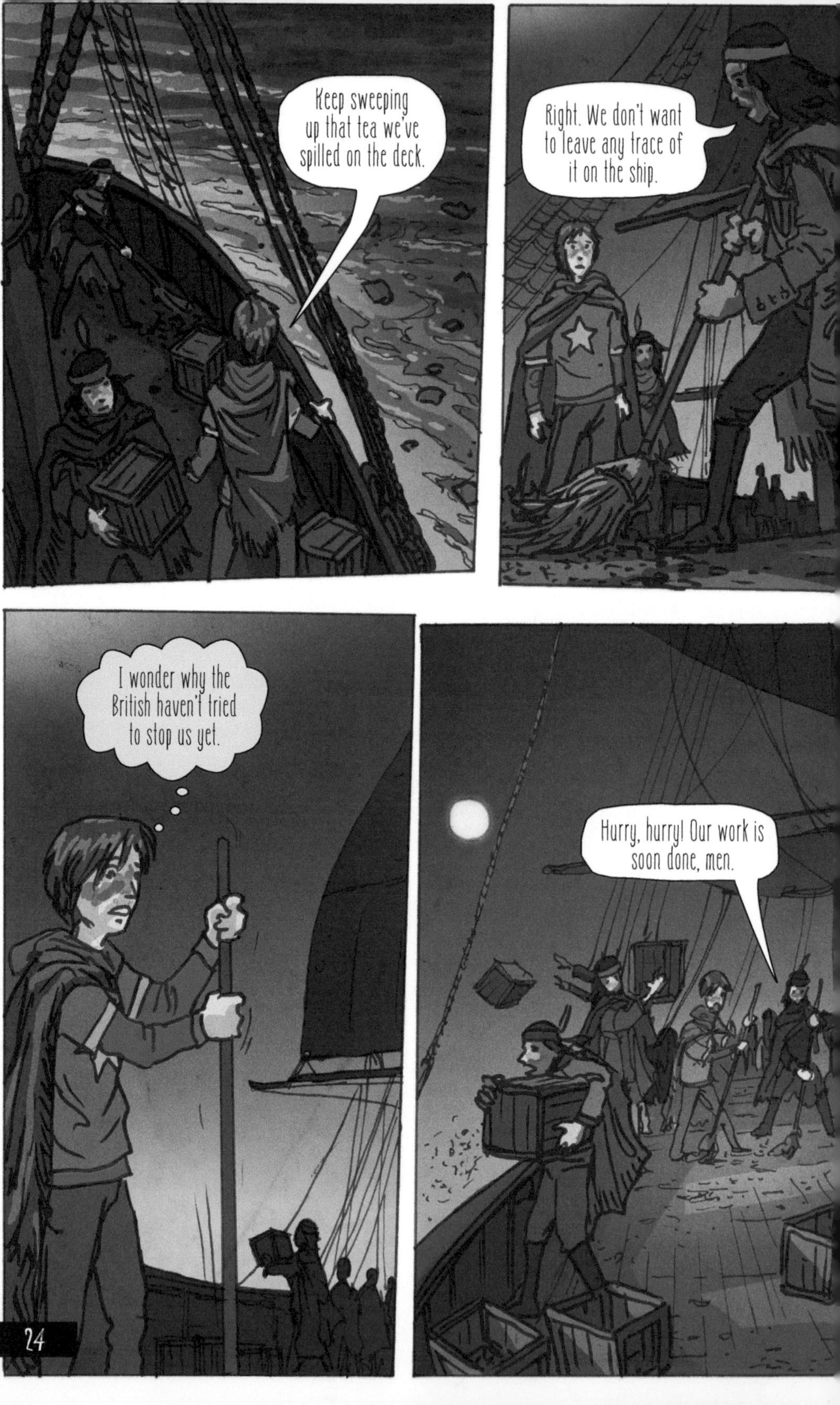

Keep sweeping up that tea we've spilled on the deck.
Right. We don't want to leave any trace of it on the ship.
I wonder why the British haven't tried to stop us yet.
Hurry, hurry! Our work is soon done, men.

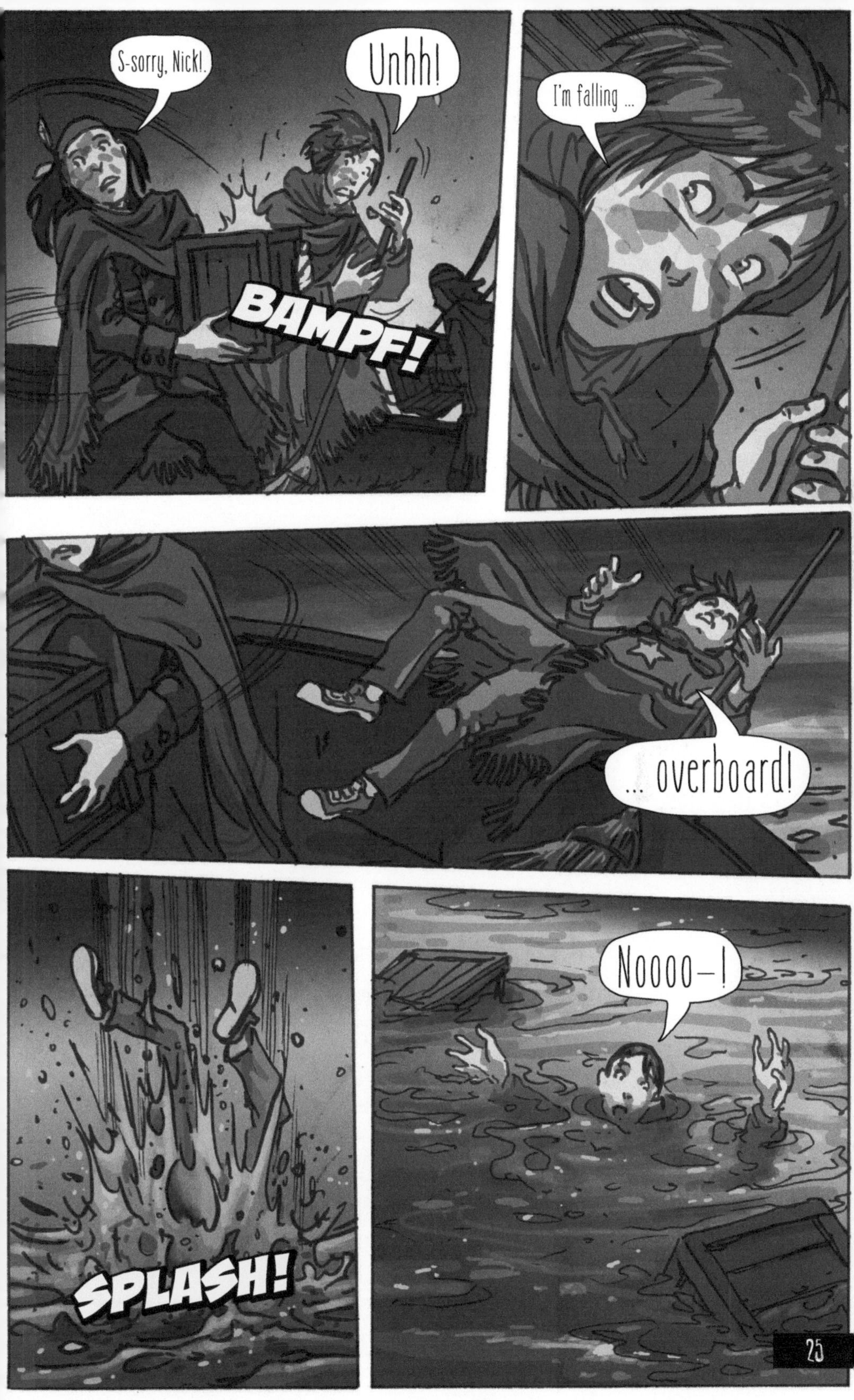
S-sorry, Nick!
Unhh!
BAMPF!
I'm falling ...
... overboard!
SPLASH!
Noooo—!

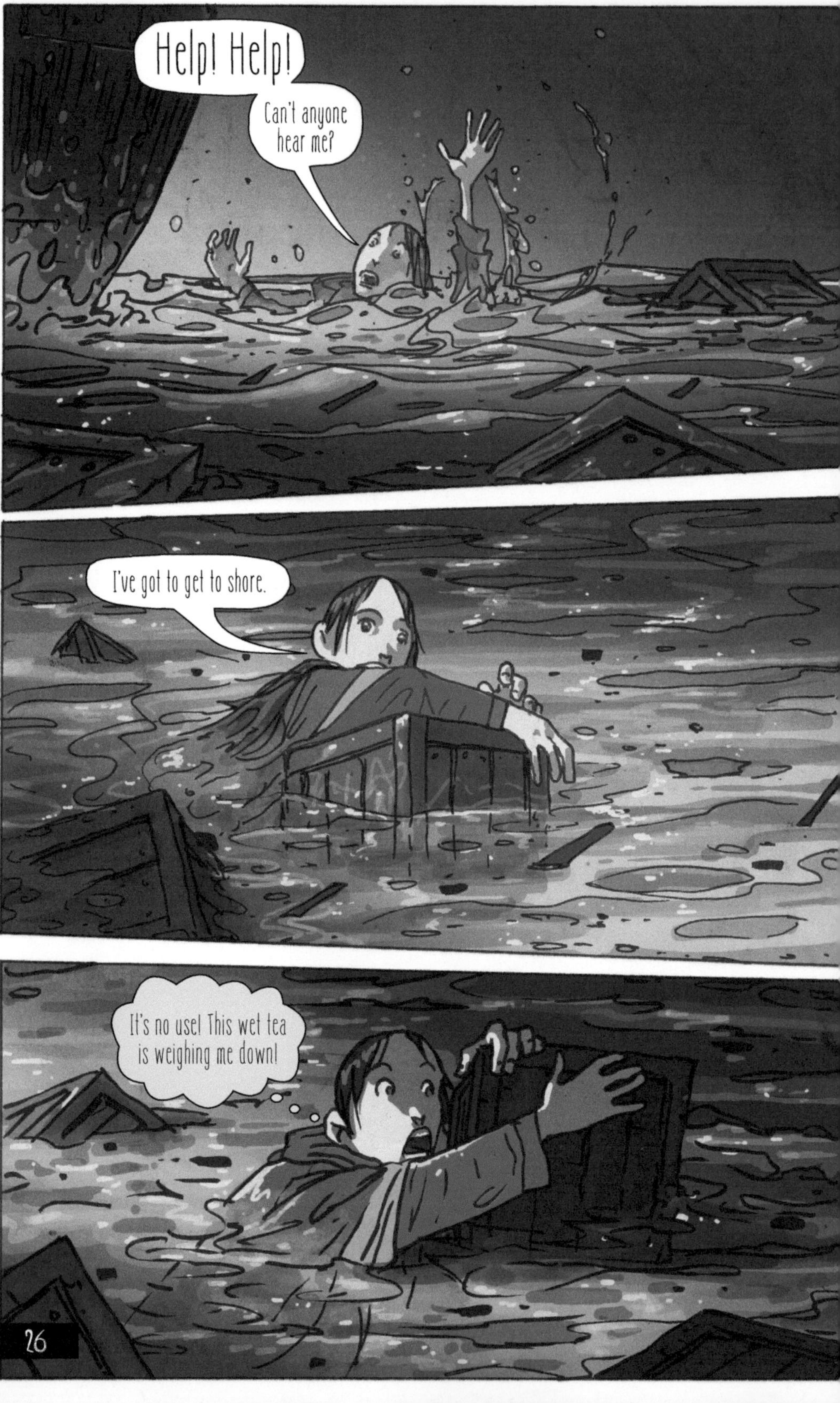
Help! Help!
Can't anyone hear me?
I've got to get to shore.
It's no use! This wet tea is weighing me down!

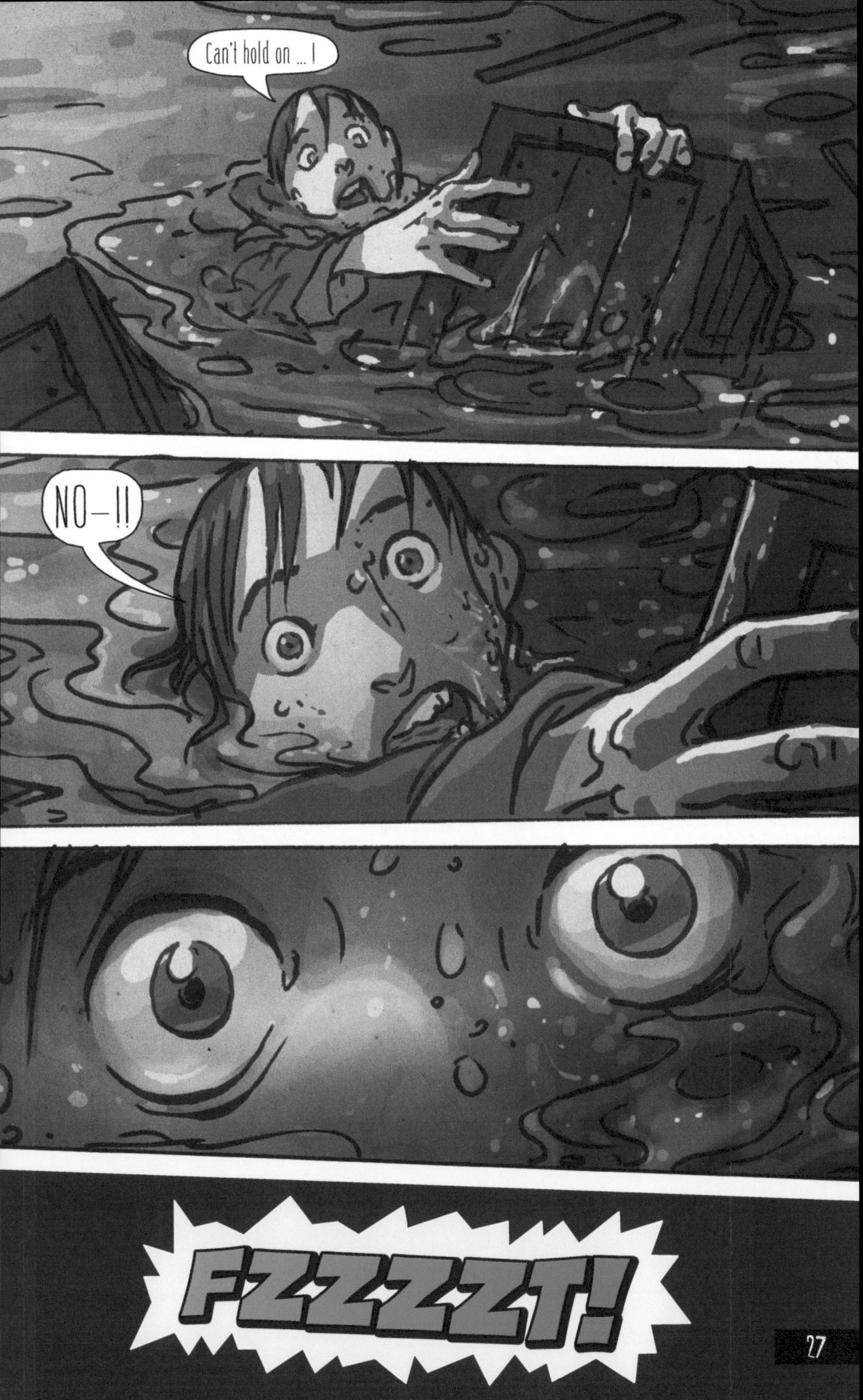
Can't hold on ... !
NO—!!
FZZZZT!

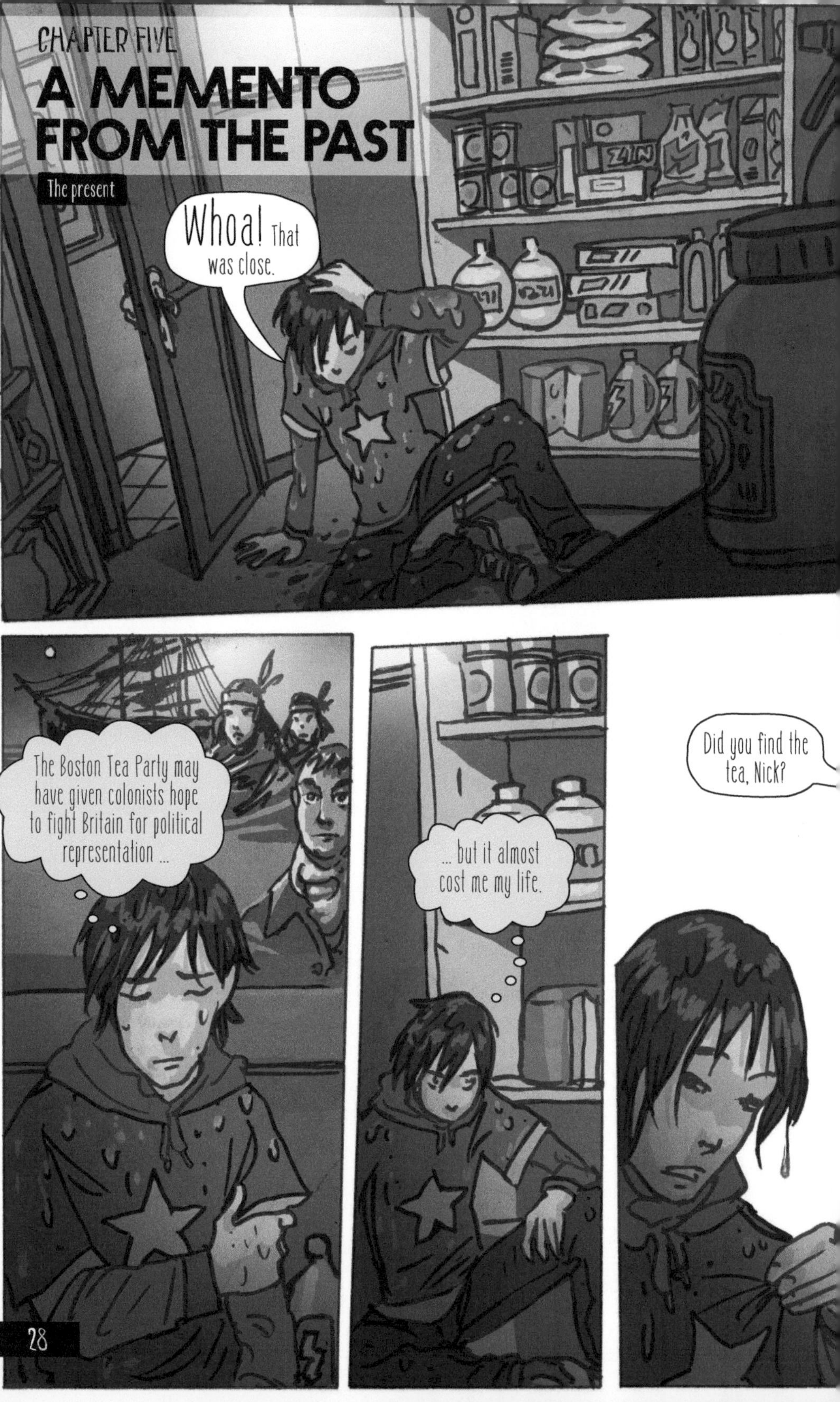
CHAPTER FIVE
A MEMENTO FROM THE PAST
The present
Whoa! That was close.
The Boston Tea Party may have given colonists hope to fight Britain for political representation ...
... but it almost cost me my life.
Did you find the tea, Nick?

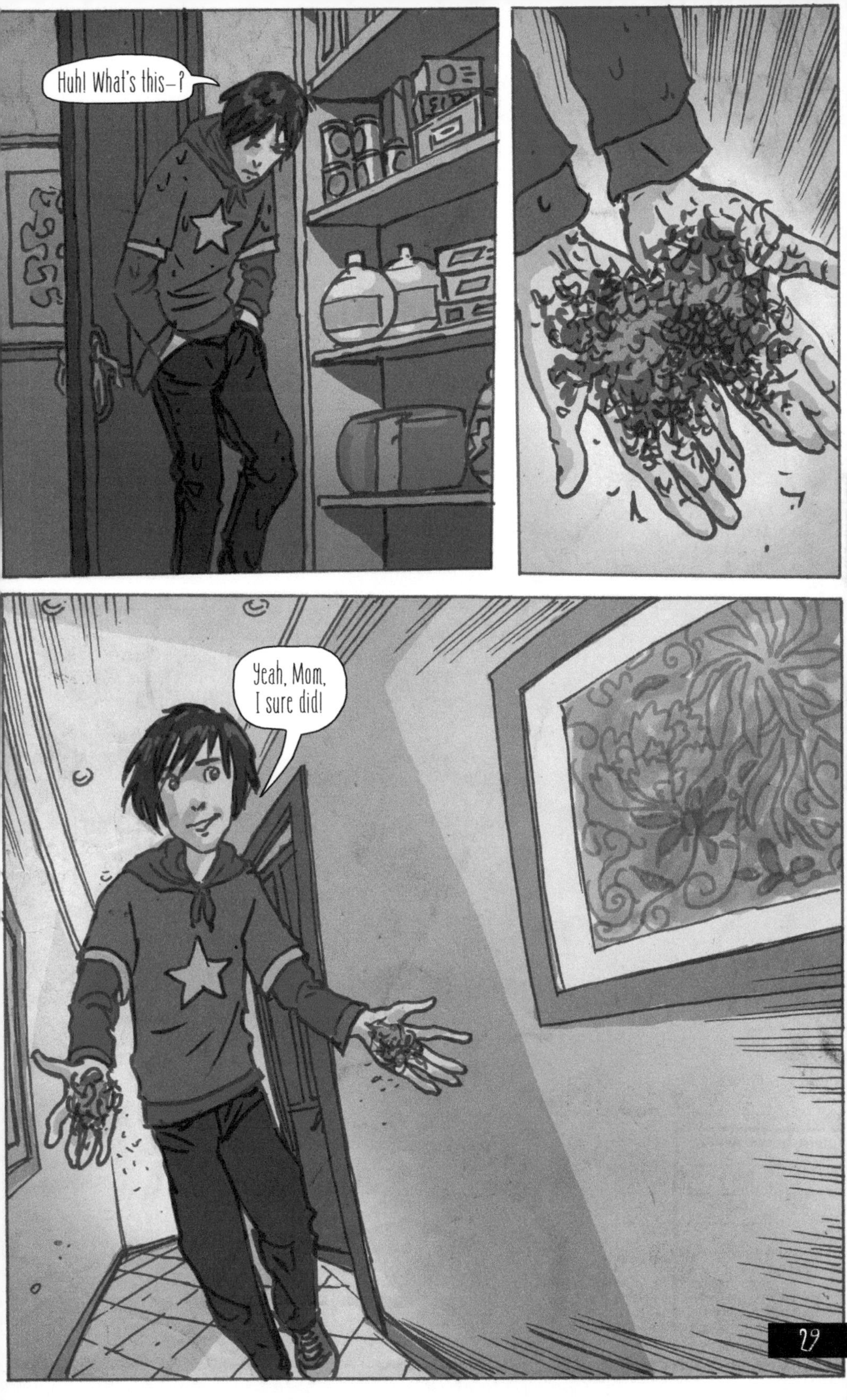

Huh! What's this—?
Yeah, Mom, I sure did!

FLUX FILES

FRENCH AND INDIAN WAR

The war fought between the British and the French in America is called the French and Indian War (1754-1763). American Indian groups fought for both sides in the conflict. Britain won the war and established itself as the main colonial power in the eastern part of North America.

TEA POPULARITY

Tea was as important to the colonists as coffee is to adults today. Everyone drank it—rich and poor, young and old. It was easy to make and transport. By the 1760s, the total population of the colonies was only about 1.6 million people. But Americans were using 1.2 million tons (1 million metric tons) of tea each year!

BRITISH INACTION

British authorities in Boston did nothing to stop the Tea Party. Admiral John Montagu, commander of the British Navy, saw what was happening from his house near Griffin's Wharf. Officers and sailors aboard the British gunship in Boston Harbor also watched the destruction of the tea. The British claimed that they could not break up the protestors without shooting into the crowd and thereby injuring innocent bystanders.

MORE TEA PARTIES

Other tea parties took place in New York, New Jersey, and Maryland shortly after the one in Boston. A second tea party occurred in Boston on March 7, 1774.

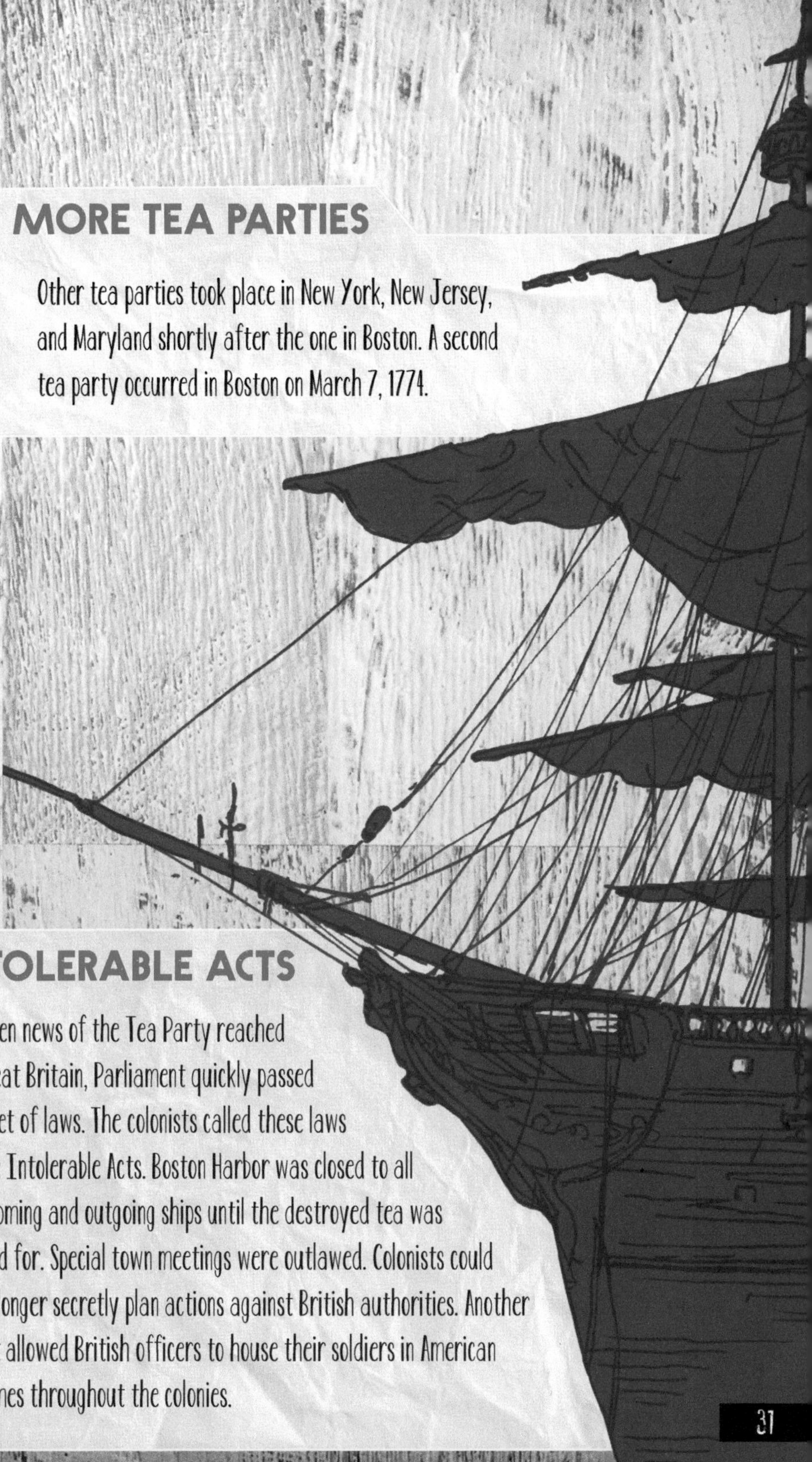

INTOLERABLE ACTS

When news of the Tea Party reached Great Britain, Parliament quickly passed a set of laws. The colonists called these laws the Intolerable Acts. Boston Harbor was closed to all incoming and outgoing ships until the destroyed tea was paid for. Special town meetings were outlawed. Colonists could no longer secretly plan actions against British authorities. Another act allowed British officers to house their soldiers in American homes throughout the colonies.

GLOSSARY

BYSTANDER (BYE-stan-dur)—someone who is at a place where something happens to someone else

CARGO (KAHR-goh)—the goods carried by a ship, vehicle, or aircraft

COLONIST (KAH-luh-nist)—a person who settles in a new territory that is governed by his or her home country

COLONY (KAH-luh-nee)—a place that is settled by people from another country and is controlled by that country

CUSTOMS AGENT (KUHS-tuhms AY-juhnt)—a government official who collects taxes and gives permission for ships to enter or leave a country

DUTY (DOO-tee)—a tax or charge on goods brought into a country

EXPORT (EK-sport)—to send and sell goods to other countries

IMPORT (IM-port)—to bring goods into one country from another

INTOLERABLE (in-TOL-ur-uh-buhl)—difficult to endure

PARLIAMENT (PAHR-luh-muhnt)—the group of British people who have been elected to make the laws in Great Britain

PATRIOT (PAY-tree-uht)—a person who loves and fights for his or her country

PROTEST (pro-TEST)—to object to something strongly and publicly

REPRESENTATION (rep-ri-zen-TAY-shuhn)—the right of being represented by someone, especially in the legislature of a government

TAX (TAKS)—money collected from a country's citizens to help pay for running the government

TYRANNY (TIHR-uh-nee)—a cruel or unfair government in which all power is in the hands of a single ruler

READ MORE

CUNNINGHAM, KEVIN. *The Boston Tea Party*. Cornerstones of Freedom. Danbury, Conn.: Children's Press, 2013.

GONDOSCH, LINDA. *How Did Tea and Taxes Spark a Revolution? and Other Questions About the Boston Tea Party*. Six Questions of American History. Minneapolis: Lerner Publications, 2011.

PERRITANO, JOHN. *The Causes of the American Revolution*. Understanding the American Revolution. New York: Crabtree Publishing Company, 2013.

INTERNET SITES

FactHound offers a safe, fun way to find Internet sites related to this book. All sites on FactHound have been researched by our staff.

Here's all you do:

Visit *www.facthound.com*

Type in this code: 9781476539461

Super-cool stuff!

Check out projects, games and lots more at
www.capstonekids.com

INDEX

ABOUT THE AUTHOR

Nel Yomtov is a writer of children's nonfiction books and graphic novels. He specializes in writing about history, country studies, science, and biography. His graphic novel adaptation, *Jason and the Golden Fleece*, published by Stone Arch Books was a winner of the 2009 Moonbeam Children's Book Award and the 2011 Lighthouse Literature Award. Nel is an avid American military history buff and has written two additional graphic novels for Capstone, *True Stories of World War I* and *True Stories of the Civil War*. He lives in the New York City area.

MORE NICKOLAS FLUX ADVENTURES

ARRESTED FOR WITCHCRAFT!
NICKOLAS FLUX
AND THE SALEM WITCH TRIALS

DEFEND UNTIL DEATH!
NICKOLAS FLUX
AND THE BATTLE OF THE ALAMO

Night of Rebellion!
NICKOLAS FLUX
AND THE BOSTON TEA PARTY

STAKE A CLAIM!
NICKOLAS FLUX
AND THE CALIFORNIA GOLD RUSH

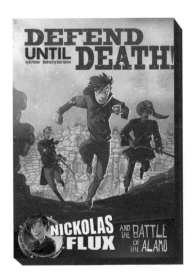